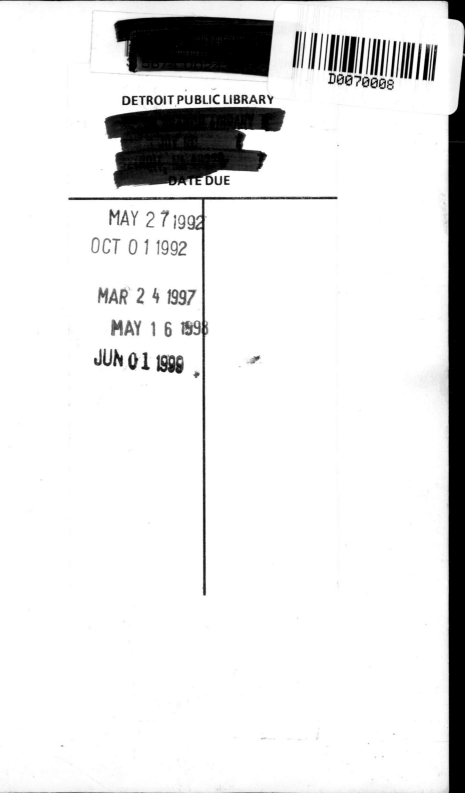

D0070008

Butterflies
and Moths
HOW THEY FUNCTION

Butterflies are undoubtedly among the most beautiful inverte-brates we have. These are a monarch, above, and a queen butterfly.

Butterflies and Moths

HOW THEY FUNCTION

Dorothy Hinshaw Patent

HOLIDAY HOUSE · *New York*

*For scientists whose love of lepidopterans
has led to the discovery of
important biological principles*

Library of Congress Cataloging in Publication Data

Patent, Dorothy Hinshaw.
  Butterflies and moths, how they function.

  Includes index.
  SUMMARY: Discusses the anatomy, physiology,
habits, and behavior of a group of insects both
harmful and beneficial to man.
    1. Lepidoptera—Juvenile literature.
[1. Butterflies. 2. Moths] I. Title.
QL544.2.P37   595.7'8   78–20614
ISBN 0–8234–0350–5

Contents

Butterflies and flowers make one of the great "teams" in nature; the insect sucks out nourishment and meanwhile leaves behind the fertilizing pollen from the last flower, starting the seed-producing process. This is a painted beauty, Vanessa virginiensis, *on a purple aster.*

1 · *Flutter, Flap, and Glide . . .*

Butterflies are among the most familiar creatures around us. Even in big cities, vacant lots and parks are graced by the gentle flight of familiar butterflies— monarchs, cabbage butterflies, perhaps a red admiral or a painted lady. We are accustomed to moths as well, although we may not look at them in such a friendly way. Moths are creatures that eat our clothes, infest our trees and crops, and flutter at us unexpectedly when we open the front door after dark. But like most distinctions that people try to make in nature, this image of butterflies as harmless, pretty daytime fliers and moths as somewhat sinister creatures of the night is not strictly true. There are butterflies which can be considered as enemies of humans, such as the cabbage butterfly, and moths which are great friends, like the silkworm moth. Quite a few moths fly by day, and some rival butterflies in their beauty. For both butterflies and moths, called collectively by scientists the Lepidoptera, lead a much greater variety

9

of lives than most people realize.

There are more kinds of butterflies and moths than of any other sort of insect except beetles. Moth species far outnumber butterflies; while about 111,000 kinds of moths are known, 24,000 butterflies have been described. Butterflies range in size from the very small pigmy blue found in southern California, which is less than a half-inch across, to the giant female Queen Alexandra's birdwing of New Guinea, which measures about 25 centimeters (some ten inches) from wing tip to wing tip. While some giant silk moths rival the birdwings in size, the smallest moths are only a quarter the size of the little pigmy blues. Lepidopterans are found throughout the world where animals can survive, from the arctic regions to the tropics, on islands and atop mountains.

While a few thousand butterfly and moth species live in the United States, by far the greatest variety of species live in the tropics. There are several reasons for this abundance of tropical lepidopterans. Butterflies and moths are small creatures which cannot keep their bodies warm the way we can. When they live in an area where winters are cold, they must spend several months tucked away in a sheltered spot, awaiting the arrival of spring. Some wait out winter as eggs, some as caterpillars, still others as pupae, and a few as adults. But butterflies and moths of many families have never been able to adapt to cold winter conditions. These kinds are unable to survive in Europe and

North America, where winters are cold.

Butterflies and moths depend on plants for food, and their caterpillars are often quite specialized in their choice of diet. The tropics offer an amazing variety of plants as food. The more different kinds of food plants in an area, the more different kinds of plant-eaters can be accommodated. Tropical jungles are very different from our familiar forests in another important way, aside from their much greater variety of plant life. In a northern forest, an animal may be adapted for life in the trees or life on the ground. But the plants in tropical forests grow so thickly and at so many heights that there are many different layers through which living things can move. This division of the tropical forest into many distinct layers increases still further the variety of animals which can live there.

Different Life Styles

Many butterflies live only a few short days as adults. They emerge from their pupae, mate, lay their eggs, and die. Most kinds feed on nectar from flowers to sustain themselves during their few days of flight. But quite a few species have longer adult lives. The familiar monarch may live for many months and fly thousands of kilometers during its migration. Many tropical butterflies have a long life span, too, and are able to learn the landmarks of their home areas with surprising accuracy. Many of these long-lived butter-flies gain nourishment from rotten fruit, puddles of urine, or even from pollen, in addition to feeding on nectar.

One very successful family of butterflies, the blues (Lycaenidae), almost always live in association with ants. While some blues merely frequent the same tree trunks as do ants, others cannot survive without them. Butterflies in another family closely related to blues, metalmarks (Rionidae) also live in close proximity to ants.

Moth lives are more varied than those of butterflies. Moth larvae may inhabit unexpected places such as beehives and rushing streams. Many moths fly very little, while the sphinxes and hawkmoths (Sphingidae) rival hummingbirds in their flying ability. Some adult moths do not feed at all, but others have surprising habits such as attacking the eyes of cattle or sucking blood like mosquitoes.

Butterfly or Moth?

If you look at a typical American lepidopteran, you can easily classify it as a butterfly or moth. The most obvious difference between the two groups is that most butterflies close their wings together above their bodies, while most moths lay theirs flat or fold them at a roof angle across their backs, with the forewings on top. Butterflies generally have slim, smooth-looking bodies while moths have thicker, often furry-looking ones. There are exceptions to these general rules, however. Many day-flying moths hold their wings the way butterflies do, and skipper butterflies have thick, hairy bodies and sometimes fold their wings in a mothlike manner. (Some scientists actually consider skippers to be as closely related to moths as to butterflies.)

The most reliable difference between the two groups lies in the antennae. Butterfly antennae usually have knobs on the ends; few moth antennae do. Moth antennae may have quite elaborate branching shapes, but almost always lack the distinctive butterfly knobs. Another difference often cited is that moths make cocoons, while butterflies do not. But all caterpillars can spin silk, and some butterfly caterpillars spin simple cocoons. Many moth caterpillars, on the other hand, dig underground to pupate and do not spin cocoons at all.

Lepidopterans as Insects

Butterflies and moths are typical highly developed insects. Like those of all insects, their bodies are divided into three sections called the head, thorax, and abdomen, and they have six legs attached to the thorax. The insect body is organized in a very different way from the familiar vertebrate one. While we have our skeletons on the insides of our bodies, insects have theirs on the outside. Their "exoskeleton" serves the same functions of body support and muscle attachment as does our "endoskeleton," but it also provides insects with a protective armor. The soft, living parts of the body are held safely inside of the hard, outer covering called the cuticle. It is this firm, nonliving cuticle which makes butterfly collecting a possible hobby. When a butterfly dies, its soft insides rot or dry up, but the shape of its body is retained by its outer covering.

While a hard exoskeleton has its advantages, it also creates problems for insects. Because it is encased in a solid, nonliving covering, an insect can grow only by shedding its cuticle (a process called molting) and producing a new, larger one. Thus insect growth does not appear to be gradual, like ours. A young insect grows until its skin is tight. Then it sheds the old cuticle and swells up with air or water while its skin cells secrete a new cuticle. This pattern of growth and molting continues until the insect reaches its final adult size. Then it stops growing and does not molt again.

Insect bodies are different on the inside, too. Mammals breathe with lungs. Inside the lungs, many minute blood vessels close to the inner lung surface pick up oxygen from the air. A chemical called hemoglobin, located in the red blood cells, carries the oxygen to the body tissues. Insects have a completely different way of distributing oxygen to the body. Instead of lungs, they have a complicated system of air tubes called tracheae, which carry air directly from the outside of the body into the interior of the animal. In many of the larger insects, air is in effect pumped into and out of the tracheae through openings in the body called spiracles. The tracheae branch into microscopic air tubes called tracheoles which are filled at their ends with fluid. The oxygen from the air dissolves in this liquid and is then picked up by the body cells. The liquid helps keep the cells from drying out.

Because they have this other system for obtaining oxygen, insects do not need a well-developed circulatory system with a strong heart and branching blood vessels such as vertebrates have. Their blood system is much less complicated. The heart is merely a tube which is open at the front end. Blood enters the heart through slits in its sides. When the heart contracts, the slits close and blood is forced forward through the front end of the heart to the brain. From there, the blood flows through the body spaces and bathes all the internal organs. This is called an "open circulatory system," since the blood is not enclosed inside definite blood vessels.

The nervous system of insects is quite different from ours, too. The brain of mammals is so important that if it is damaged, the animal may die. But the insect brain does not have such nearly complete control over the body. Even if its entire head is removed, an insect can continue to live for quite a while. Inside the insect body are masses of nerve cells called ganglia (singular, ganglion). The ganglia play important roles in controlling body functions. Mammals have ganglia, too, but they are not as independent of the brain as are the ganglia of insects.

Becoming an Adult Insect

Insects have two different ways of getting from egg to adult. Some, like grasshoppers, change gradually as they grow and molt. The young grasshopper may lack wings and have rather short legs, but it is easily recognizable as a grasshopper. But who would guess to look at a fat, short-legged caterpillar that it would grow up to be a slim, long-legged, graceful butterfly? The word "metamorphosis" is used to describe the changes leading from the young stage of an animal to the adult. Insects such as cockroaches and grasshoppers, which undergo a gradual change, are said to have "incomplete metamorphosis." Those such as flies, bees, and butterflies, which show a striking change from a wormlike larva to a winged adult, have "complete metamorphosis."

Insects with complete metamorphosis do all their growing and most of their feeding as larvae. The larva is a specialized feeding machine, well adapted for the job of cramming in as much food as efficiently as possible. The adult, on the other hand, is adapted mainly for reproduction. While some butterflies have a long adult life, many moths are so short-lived that they lack

A lepidopteran in the caterpillar stage in many cases sticks to one kind of plant for feeding, like this monarch caterpillar munching on a milkweed leaf.

usable mouthparts. All feeding is done during the caterpillar stage, and the adult moth must live on food reserves built up by the larva.

While this type of life cycle may seem strange, it has definite advantages. The larva can concentrate completely on its job of eating, with its body especially adapted to that job. If the adults do feed, they do not compete for food with their offspring, since they drink nectar or feed on rotting fruit, while the caterpillars eat leaves. The adult insect need feed only enough to stay alive, since it does not grow. It can concentrate its energies on finding a mate and laying eggs, without spending a lot of time eating.

Lepidopteran Families

While the huge number of lepidopteran species may seem bewildering, certain kinds show obvious similarities to one another and are arranged into groups called families. Just as animals in the cat family, such as lions, cheetahs, and leopards, share certain characteristics, lepidopterans in any one family have key resemblances. The scientists who study insects, called entomologists, do not always agree on the arrangement of butterfly and moth families, however. For example, many place most butterflies into one huge family, the Nymphalidae, which they then divide into smaller subfamilies. This can get very confusing, so in this book all these distinct groups, such as the wood

Every family of lepidopterans has its own characteristics. These are pierid butterflies, family Pieridae, which often swarm in great numbers and then settle together on a moist sandbank to drink (or even on wet laundry).

nymphs (Satyridae) and the milkweed butterflies (Danaidae) will be called families. Using this arrangement, there are up to 15 butterfly families.

Skippers (Hesperiidae) are the most mothlike butterflies. They have thick bodies and some hold their wings flat along their sides the way moths do. Skippers are a common sight, darting across the lawn and resting on dandelion blossoms. Butterflies in the family Pieridae are among the most familiar. These include the cabbage butterfly and the bright yellow sulphurs. The white and yellow colors of these insects are produced by different pigments than in other butterflies. Because of their short caterpillar life, whites and sulphurs can produce several generations during one summer. Swallowtails, members of the family Papilionidae, are easy to recognize by the characteristic "tails" on their hindwings. This family also includes the largest butterflies in the world, the birdwings. The females of some birdwings have a wingspan of over 25 centimeters (about ten inches), while the males are smaller. The large white Parnassus butterflies, with their black and red spots, also belong to this family.

By one scheme of classification, there are close to 70 different moth families. Many moths are small and inconspicuous, but some are quite familiar. One of the largest moth families is the Geometridae. Inchworms and loopers, named for their unique way of getting around, are geometrid caterpillars. Many loopers are serious crop pests. Adult geometrids tend to fly during the daytime and have strong wings. The hawkmoths and sphinx moths (Sphingidae) are also well known. They fly like hummingbirds and feed from the same sorts of flowers as hummingbirds do, hovering in front of the blooms and sucking nectar. Some crop pests, such as the tobacco or tomato hornworm, are sphinx moth caterpillars. You may be lucky enough to have seen the large and striking cynthia or cecropia moths (Saturniidae), also called giant silkworm moths, with their beautifully patterned wings. The tent caterpillar moths (Lasiocampidae) are much better known from their colony-making caterpillars than from the plain brown or gray moths. Tent caterpillars can quickly devastate a tree with their voracious appetites.

This is just a small sample of lepidopteran families. With so many different ones, it is impossible to become familiar with them all. But several more of the most interesting families will be introduced along the way.

2 · Courtship and Mating

The chief business of the adult lepidopteran is reproduction. Many kinds live only long enough to mate and lay eggs. While there are many variations in ways to find a mate, there is a basic "butterfly pattern" and a basic "'moth pattern." Unfortunately, watching the courtship and mating of lepidopterans is not easy because of their small size and their ability to fly. Since most moths mate in the dark, they are especially difficult to study.

While the males and females of most lepidopterans look virtually identical, some kinds have striking differences between the sexes. Male brimstones (Pieridae) are bright yellow, while females are a whitish green. Male promethea moths have largely black wings, while the females are marked with brown and pale maroon. The most striking sex differences to our eyes are those of the morphos of tropical America. Several species have inconspicuous, dull brown females and brilliant, iridescent blue or green males.

Male and female whites and sulphurs look the same to us. But scientists have found that to a butterfly's eyes, they are very different. The scales on the wings of many male sulphurs reflect ultraviolet light, creating an iridescence of equal brilliance to that of the brilliant blue morphos, but at wavelengths which are invisible to the human eye. Male whites, such as the common cabbage butterfly, also have ultraviolet colors which are invisible to us. Both species can see ultraviolet light, however, and males use the flashing wings as a way of telling males from females.

When the two sexes are identical, an experienced person may still be able to distinguish them. The female's abdomen is likely to be rounder than the male's, and the male has claspers at the end of his abdomen. Many male butterflies also have special patches of scent scales which form dark spots on their wings.

Butterflies and moths are basically solitary creatures, with few exceptions. Finding a mate could be a chancy affair for animals which may live widely separated. Butterflies and moths have solved the problems of mate-finding in very different ways. Butterflies, being creatures of the day, rely largely on sight to find mates, while moths use scent.

Hit or Miss

Walking through the woods on a sunny day, you might notice butterflies perched in the spots of dappled sunlight on the ground. These butterflies are not just taking a sunbath, for they are males on the lookout for passing females. They will fly out at anything vaguely resembling a butterfly, such as a falling leaf. If the fluttering object happens to be another male, the two butterflies flutter upward together, spiraling around one another. They quickly separate, and the first male returns to his sun patch. Each male guards his particular area of brightness from intruders as it moves along the ground with the sun until he spots and successfully pursues a female. Any vacant sun patches are quickly taken over by other males which have been flying about the treetops looking for mates.

This pattern is typical for butterflies. The perches may be on hedges or in grass instead of in the woods, but in general, male butterflies search for the females either from their sunny perches or by flying about actively. Some species increase their chances by perching on the food plant where the females will eventually lay her eggs. But it is all a hit-or-miss affair, with the males tirelessly pursuing every passing flutter until they find mates.

The Queen and the Monarch

One butterfly, the queen, has been thoroughly studied by determined scientists led by Drs. Lincoln and Jane Brower. They used film and patient observation to unravel the queen's secrets. A male queen has small brushes called hairpencils which he can protrude from the tip of his abdomen. When he spots a flying female, he overtakes her in the air. As they fly together, he moves to a position in front of and above her. He then brushes her head with his hairpencils. The hairpencils deposit microscopic bits of dust on the female's antennae. These bits of dust contain two chemicals. One calms the female, making her alight on the nearby plants, while the other acts as a glue which attaches the particles to her antennae. After she has landed, he hovers in front of her, brushing more dust onto her antennae. If she is ready to mate, the female folds her wings above her body. He lands on her, grasping the side of her wings with his legs. He then curves his abdomen around and links it to hers. Once successfully mated, the male flies off, carrying the quiet female beneath him, to a less conspicuous place among the shrubbery. There they remain together for several hours.

The monarch butterfly is a close relative of the queen. While males have hairpencils, they are small and of little importance in courtship. The male monarch perches in an obvious spot, usually in the sun, waiting for females. He flies at all passing monarchs and some other butterflies as well, but gives up quickly if the insect pursued is not a female monarch. If it is a female, he nudges her with his body, and she flies rapidly upward, with him in hot pursuit. This fast, upward flight may last over a minute, and the

The extended hairpencils of a male queen, Danaus gilippus
berenice. *These delicate fibers play an important part in courting.*

butterflies may end up a hundred feet above ground. Then the male suddenly pounces on the back of the female. He repeats this pouncing, forcing her to fly downward. Eventually he manages to grab her body, wrapping his legs around her wings. Now she is trapped and, although she struggles to fly, she cannot. The male spreads his wings so that the pair soars gently down together. After landing, the male attaches his abdomen to hers and flies off with his mate to a secluded place. Many male monarchs do use their hairpencils during courtship, but successful grabbing of the female's wings is much more important. If the hairpencils of a monarch are removed, he can still mate successfully. But a male queen without hairpencils hasn't a chance with the opposite sex.

Interacting with Plants

During their studies of the queen, the Browers made a curious discovery. While female butterflies reared in captivity were perfectly successful at mating, laboratory-reared males were not, even when raised on their normal food plant. Studies of a related butterfly, the African queen, revealed that if laboratory-reared males were allowed access to plants containing certain kinds of chemicals, they soon possessed the normal hairpencil chemicals. These puzzling facts may be partly explained by some very recent discoveries about some tropical butterflies. The gathering of butterflies, especially males, around certain plants has long been noticed. Chemicals released when the plants are damaged or dying attract great numbers of butterflies which feed on the dead shoots. The butterflies gorge themselves by drinking up droplets of liquid on the plant surface. If the plant is dry, a butterfly will regurgitate droplets of fluid, spread it out with his long, extended mouth (called the proboscis), and suck it up again. Some become so full they can barely fly and may stay on the plant as long as six hours.

When the butterflies are examined, most turn out to be males belonging to two families, the milkweed butterflies (Danaidae) and the closely related ithomiids (Ithomiidae). In one study, over 3000 individuals of 80 species were collected, and 97 per cent were males. Thus it appears that male butterflies need something that these plants provide. The hairpencils of male danaids contain chemicals quite similar to those in the plants; apparently they need to gather their supply of raw material from the plants, for their bodies seem unable to make them.

What about the male ithomiids? Their situation turns out to be more complicated. These butterflies do not have hairpencils like those of danaids. Instead, they have clusters of long hairs on the front edges of their hindwings. These can be held down and covered by the front wings in flight. But a mate-seeking male will sit in a sunny spot with the hairs uncovered and spread out. Many ithomiids normally stay in the dark forest. Their wings are largely transparent, with some white and black markings. While flitting through the dappled forest light, these butterflies are very inconspicuous.

But when sitting in the sun on a leaf, they are a brilliant sight. The sun shines off the transparent areas of the wings, causing brilliant flashes of color which contrast strongly with the white markings and dark veins on the wings. If another butterfly flies by, the male ithomiid dashes after it, just like the males of other butterflies. But if the other butterfly is a male, it is repelled by the odor of the chemical released from the wing hairs. All the male ithomiids observed produce the same chemical, and all were repelled by it. The wing brushes of these butterflies are used to repel possible rivals and recognize males rather than to subdue females. Since many of these species are very similar in appearance, confusion could be easy. But by being able to recognize other males quickly, the mate-searching male avoids wasting more energy on fruitless flights than necessary.

Alluring Aromas

Butterflies rely on both sight and scent to find and identify their mates. But most moths use odor alone, for they are largely night-active creatures. The attraction system used by moths is especially efficient.

One of the plumelike antennae of a luna moth, Actias luna. *Male moth antennae often, not invariably, have such shapes and are wonderfully sensitive to the female's attractant odor.*

The female moth, usually shortly after emerging from her cocoon, releases a chemical attractant into the air. The antennae of male moths are very sensitive to this attractant. In many moth species, the female has simple antennae, while the male's antennae are beautiful plumes. They are studded with special sensory hairs which react to the female attractant and stimulate the male to turn into the wind and fly off in search of her. The antennae of the male silkworm moth have up to 16,000 of these hairs each. Female moth antennae in most species lack them entirely. The sex attractant of some moths is so potent that it can lure males from five miles away. That's quite a distance for a moth to fly.

Females of some moths cannot even fly. Bagworms (Psychidae) interweave their silk with leaves and twigs, producing protective bag "houses" for themselves. They become pupae inside the bags. When the male moths emerge, they fly off to look for females. The female has no wings, legs, antennae, or eyes. She cannot eat. But she does produce a sex attractant which draws the male to her. After mating, the female lays her eggs right there inside her own bag, where they spend the winter protected.

Much like butterflies, some male moths produce chemicals which calm the females after they are located. The male Indian meal moth has scent glands on the front edges of his forewings. If these glands are removed, the female moth will not remain still long enough to mate with the male.

Moth sex attractants are being studied by many scientists, for they offer an improved way of controlling pests. Traps containing sex attractants are set out in fields to find out if any moths of a particular pest species are present. If they are absent, the farmer need not waste pesticides by spraying his crops. But if the pest appears, he will spray to kill it. The first sex attractant "pesticide" has been licensed. This new and safer way of controlling insects took years to develop. Tiny, thin plastic tubes containing the sex attractant of the pink bollworm moth are dropped into a cotton field. They release the sex attractant slowly into the air, so that it is in the air everywhere. Male moths in search of females get thoroughly confused, for they cannot follow an odor trail to a female. The chemical is identical to that produced by the female moths; with the scent all around them the males lose their clue to the location of females and fail to mate, eliminating the next generation of moths.

Scientists hope to develop similar controls for other insect pests, such as gypsy moths, which also use sex attractants in their courtship. Such techniques are by far preferable to pesticides. While pesticides kill helpful as well as harmful insects, sex attractants are completely harmless chemicals which kill no creatures and only affect the particular pest which uses them. Quite a few problems still exist in developing more sex attractant controls, however. Some moths respond to the attractants only at a particular time of day or night, and some only to concentrations within a limited range. Often the sex attractant is not a single chemical compound but rather a mixture of two or more chemicals in a certain proportion. In order to attract the moths, the artificial mixture must be just like the natural one.

3 · *The Egg and What*
Hatches from It

Once mating is over, the male lepidopteran has finished his business on earth. He may die soon or live on for a while. But the female must survive for a while longer, long enough to find the proper place to deposit her precious contribution to the next generation. A female lepidopteran may lay her eggs hours or even days after mating. The sperm are passed into her body in a compact packet called a spermatophore. They are then stored in a special chamber which opens into the egg passageway. As the female lays her eggs, sperm are released to fertilize them.

A few butterflies whose caterpillars feed on grass or other very numerous plants merely scatter their eggs as they fly along, but most butterflies are very particular where they put them. If the caterpillars will hatch and begin to feed right away, the female will lay her eggs right on the leaves they eat. If the caterpillars will hatch out after overwintering in the eggs, however, she will choose a protected spot near where the leaves will be the next spring. If you watch a butterfly in a meadow, you may see her flit from plant to plant, touching down lightly for a second and then flying off. The chances are that this is a female searching for the right food plant on which to lay her eggs. Since most lepidopterans are quite specific about which plants they will eat as caterpillars, the females cannot afford to make mistakes when they lay their eggs.

The female lands on a promising leaf and drums it delicately, "tasting" it briefly with chemically sensitive receptors on her feet. If it is the right kind of plant, she curls her abdomen around to lay a single egg on the underside. Some butterflies lay their eggs in other places, but the vast majority choose the hidden and protected underside of a leaf. A few lay their eggs in clusters, but most deposit them one at a time. Butterfly eggs are a tasty delicacy for many creatures, especially ants. By scattering her eggs around here and there, the female butterfly increases the chances that some will escape hungry enemies and hatch.

Butterfly eggs are usually green or yellow. They may be so small that they are barely visible, like those of hairstreaks. Or they may be large enough that just four will comfortably fit on a pinhead, like those of swallowtails. Some butterflies lay only a few dozen eggs during their lifetime, while others produce as

A female cecropia moth lays her eggs on a twig, cementing them down at the same time.

many as 1500. The number of eggs laid probably depends on how vulnerable the eggs and larvae are to predators. Butterfly eggs are so distinctive that a knowledgeable person can identify them just as easily as by seeing the adult insect.

An insect egg may be quite small, but it is very complicated in structure. The inner, living part of the egg is surrounded by a thin egg membrane. Cells surrounding the developing egg in the ovary secrete a

Four micropyles, or entrance holes for sperm, at the center of a petal-like pattern, show up on this gypsy moth egg, magnified about 2800 times.

thick, tough shell called the chorion, which has many layers. Over the chorion, different cells in the female's body deposit a sticky layer which anchors the egg to the leaf. As the eggs are laid, they must be fertilized by the sperm which the female has stored up since mating. There are small canals opening through minute pores in the egg surface through which the sperm can pass to reach the egg to fertilize it. Only one sperm fertilizes each egg.

Inside the Egg

An insect egg may look very inactive from the outside, but much is happening on the inside. The single fertilized egg cell is dividing into smaller cells which eventually become organized into the form of the caterpillar. All this takes energy and oxygen. The energy is present as nutritious yolk inside the egg, but the oxygen must come from the outside. The chorion must have holes big enough to let in molecules of oxygen. But, like all living things on land, the insect egg must control the loss of water, or it will dry up and die. Since the water molecule is smaller than the oxygen molecule, any hole big enough to let in oxygen is also big enough to let out water.

For this reason, the egg has only a limited number of holes through which oxygen enters. These minute holes are called aeropyles. They lead from the outside into the inner layers of the eggshell. There a meshwork of fibers traps layers of gas. These layers can be amazingly complex. The chorion of the puss moth has more than 40 separate gas-containing layers. These layers help keep water from escaping too fast through the aeropyles as well as providing areas for oxygen to come in contact with the developing embryo.

The Danger of Drowning

While the egg must guard against drying out, another big danger is that of drowning. If it had a smooth surface and became engulfed by a raindrop or dew drop, an insect egg could not get enough oxygen for its development and would die. The beautiful "sculptured" patterns on butterfly eggs which make each kind so distinctive exist largely as an adaptation for dealing with the problem of too much water. Most lepidopteran eggs have complex surface patterns of low ridges and spines. When the egg becomes submerged in water, these lumps and bumps help hold a thin layer of air against its surface. Oxygen from the water drop can pass easily into the air layer and from there into the egg, ensuring its oxygen supply.

Eggs which lack such rough surface often have aeropyles which open along the top of rather high ridges or tall spines. When the egg is submerged in a droplet, these aeropyles stick up through the water like snorkel tubes into the air. Some lepidopteran eggs seem not to be threatened by flooding, for they have

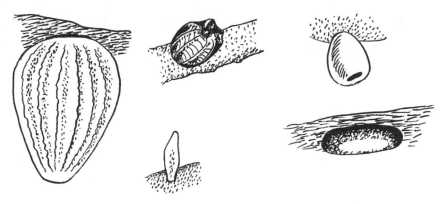

Lepidopteran eggs have many forms. From left to right, eggs of the monarch butterfly, comma butterfly (top), sulphur butterfly (bottom), io moth (top), and polyphemus moth, all greatly enlarged.

low, scattered aeropyles and smooth surfaces. Such eggs would not last long under water. Some butterfly eggs are protected from water in a different way. The tortoiseshell butterflies lay their eggs in large masses. When it rains, a bubble of air is trapped over one end of the egg mass and acts as a temporary "lung," picking up oxygen from the air and making it available to the clustered eggs.

During the egg stage no food is taken in, so there is no actual growth. As a matter of fact, since yolk is used up to provide energy for the developing embryo, the tiny caterpillar which first hatches is somewhat smaller than the original egg. During development, the material present in the single cell is reorganized and redistributed into the many cells of the caterpillar which hatches.

While some eggs hatch within three days of being

laid, others may remain in place as long as a year before the caterpillar comes out. A great number of lepidopterans pass the winter or dry season as eggs. For example, the gypsy moth lays her eggs under the bark of trees in the fall. The next spring the caterpillars hatch out. The egg reaches only a certain stage before winter sets in. Then development is suspended. Such a slowdown in metabolism, which puts an insect into a sort of "suspended animation," is called diapause. The diapause is very important to insects, for so many of them live in climates which are suitable for insect activity only during a limited part of the year. Certain climatic conditions are necessary to "wake up" the diapausing insect. Often, cold temperatures for at least a certain period of time are necessary to break the diapause. If the eggs of an insect which undergoes diapause in that stage are brought inside and never exposed to the cold, they will never hatch. Scientists who raise lepidopterans in the laboratory must know the necessary conditions for diapause and expose the eggs to them before they will produce young.

When the caterpillar is fully developed and ready to hatch, the eggshell becomes first dark, then almost transparent. The caterpillar is bathed in a layer of fluid which separates it from the shell. It drinks this fluid, swelling up its body so that it presses against the shell. Then it eats a hole in the side of the shell and pushes into the outside world.

4 · Caterpillar Life

The minute creature which hatches out of the butterfly or moth egg hardly looks promising. A barely visible speck, it immediately goes about the principal business of its life, which is eating. First it consumes the shell which protected it as it developed. Then it moves on to begin munching on the leaves of its host plant. Since most butterflies and moths lay their eggs directly on leaves of the appropriate plant, the caterpillar need not move to begin its first real meal.

It is a creature admirably adapted for a life of gluttony. Its big, strong jaws, called mandibles, have razor-sharp edges which slice off bits of leaves for chewing. Below the mandibles is a pair of maxillae, small mouthparts used to help guide food into the mouth. Its first three pairs of legs are used to hold onto its food, while the other five pairs end in suction cups which enable it to climb straight up vertical surfaces. They also have hooks on them which help the insect hang on. Inside is a large intestine which fills most of

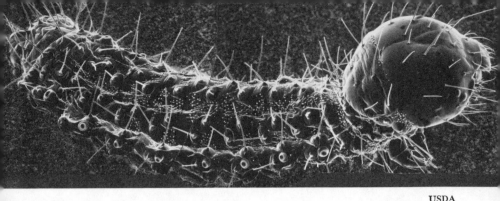

USDA

A corn earworm moth caterpillar just after hatching, as seen by the scanning electron microscope. It has not yet molted, and its actual length is less than one millimeter. A lepidopteran larva increases in size thousands of times before turning into a pupa.

the body. Here the food is digested as fast as the caterpillar eats it.

During the time between hatching and pupating (forming the pupa), the caterpillar may increase its body size by more than 30,000 times. When you realize that the caterpillar stage may last only two weeks, you can see what an enormous growth rate that is. And not only must the young insect eat enough to fuel this growth, it also must store up sufficient food to carry it through the entire pupal stage. Since the adults of some lepidopterans do not feed at all and others feed only lightly, many caterpillars also have to build up enough reserves to nourish the adult.

The Caterpillar Body

Compared to the adult butterfly, the caterpillar is a rather simple creature. Its body consists of a head plus (usually) 13 body segments. On the head are two circles of six simple eyes (ocelli) which respond to changes in light intensity but cannot form an image. It has a short pair of antennae which are chemically sensitive. The first three pairs of legs will eventually develop into the adult legs, while the other five pairs, called prolegs, are found only on the caterpillar. Eight prolegs are found along the middle of the body, while the last pair is near the hind end. The caterpillar moves by rippling waves of its body which pass from the rear end up to the front. When the muscles in the rear segments contract, the blood which bathes the internal organs is pushed forward, causing the front

The prolegs of a caterpillar—usually five per side—are stubby organs that help the long larva to get around and then disappear as it matures in the pupal form. The small true legs at front (left), just visible on this promethea moth larva, will become long and slender adult legs.　　　ALICE L. HOPF

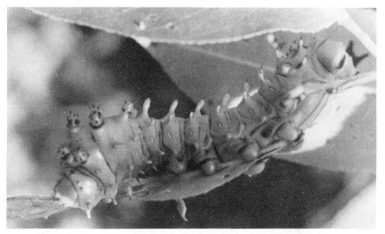

parts of the body to lengthen. The legs then grasp new positions farther forward, and muscles contract to pull up the hind end.

While it takes a great deal of imagination to see the butterfly-to-be in its caterpillar, some indications of the future flier are already there. The caterpillar head becomes the butterfly head after significant remodeling. The front part of the body bearing the first six legs becomes the butterfly's thorax, and the remainder of the body is transformed into the abdomen. But while the recognizable insect framework is there, the caterpillar's body cells in general do not become the cells of the adult. Hidden inside its body are microscopic clusters of butterfly cells—called "imaginal discs"—which do not divide and grow during larval life. Different clusters become different butterfly parts. One pair develops into the antennae, another into the front legs, still another into the wings. Thus, although the caterpillar is a fully formed, living insect, it is at the same time a walking embryo, carrying around with it the undeveloped imaginal discs which will later divide, grow, and change into the parts of the butterfly's body.

Being a Caterpillar

While its whole reason for existing is to store up energy for the adult lepidopteran which will emerge from the pupa, the caterpillar still must live its own

The portion of this queen caterpillar between the head (left) and the middle pair of protuberances will turn into the insect's thorax.

life in its own way. The caterpillar is the longest stage in the whole life cycle of many lepidopterans, and it must be especially adapted to survive in its environment. For this reason, caterpillars of closely related butterflies and moths may look different and behave very differently. Caterpillars of both the large white and the common cabbage butterfly (which are closely related) feed on cabbage leaves. The cabbage butterfly caterpillar is green and lives alone, burrowing into the heart of the cabbage after its second molt. Large white caterpillars, on the other hand, have varied colors and live in clusters. They remain on the outer leaves of the plant. The cabbage butterfly caterpillar, which is eagerly eaten by birds, is protected by both its color and its behavior. The large white caterpillar, however, tastes bad and is avoided by most birds. The bright colors act as a warning of its bad taste, apparently, and its reckless behavior is largely safe.

Unrelated caterpillars, on the other hand, may appear outwardly similar. Many edible caterpillars of both butterflies and moths are bright green and so blend in with the leaves upon which they rest. If you find a green caterpillar, it may belong to any one of a number of butterflies or moths.

Growing and Changing

Between hatching and molting to form a pupa, most caterpillars molt four times. There are thus five caterpillar stages, or instars, beginning with the tiny speck which leaves the egg. The first instar of many butter-flies is a tan creature with a black head which can eat only pinholes in food-plant leaves. Within a day or two this little larva molts for the first time. The re-sulting second instar larva possesses the special char-acteristics of its species. With a magnifying glass an experienced observer can now recognize what sort of caterpillar he is looking at.

Every time the caterpillar molts, it increases sig-nificantly in size. While its new skin is still soft, it gulps air, temporarily increasing its body size; thus there will be growing room inside when the cuticle hardens. Most living things grow through cell di-vision. More and more cells are formed in the body, and each kind of cell tends to be a certain size. But caterpillars grow by an increase in the size of their body cells instead of by increasing the number of cells. Thus the little first-instar caterpillar and the full-grown, fifth-instar caterpillar, which may be two or three inches long, have about the same number of cells in their bodies. The cells of the first instar are very small, while the fifth-instar cells are huge.

Caterpillar Foods

Leaves are by far the most usual caterpillar diet. Different caterpillars attack their food in various ways. Caterpillars of many small moths are leaf miners. They bite through the tough outer leaf layer and burrow into the softer, protected inside. Each species of leaf miner makes a characteristic type of pattern inside the leaf which can be recognized from the outside. Merely by seeing the leaf, a scientist specializing in leaf miners can recognize the responsible moth species without even seeing the caterpillar itself.

Because leaf miner patterns are so predictable, it is possible to tell which species group (genus) caused leaf mines in fossil leaves. One scientist studied 21 fossil leaf mines and was able to tell that 11 different species from seven genera had made the mines. These species came from four different moth families, all of which have living representatives. The mines were in fossil oak leaves, and close relatives of the fossil miners still attack oaks today. Thus, for millions of years, similar moths have been feeding on oak leaves.

Caterpillars are often very particular about what they eat. Some kinds feed on only one plant species, and many specialize in one or two families. Some swallowtail larvae feed on citrus trees or plants in the parsley family, such as carrots, dill, and celery. Monarchs and their relatives are called milkweed butterflies because this is their caterpillar food. Whites feed on mustard family plants, such as cabbage, broccoli, and cauliflower.

Most butterflies lay their eggs on the appropriate food plants, and caterpillars have a very specialized sense of taste which determines what they will and

Many caterpillars stick to just a few kinds of plants for their meals. This is a viceroy butterfly larva feeding on willow leaves; it also eats poplar.

will not eat. The caterpillar's maxillae may be small, but they contain the vital taste cells. There are four taste organs, two on each maxilla. Within each taste organ are four chemically sensitive cells, each of which may be quite specific. Some may be sensitive to chemicals which stimulate feeding while others respond to feeding inhibitors—those that act as a stop sign to the insect's nervous system. The caterpillar of the large white has a cell in each taste organ which is sensitive to the mustard oil chemicals in leaves. If they are present, the caterpillar will eat. Mustard oils are

found in mustard-family plants which these caterpillars eat. If leaves of other plants, or even bits of
absorbent paper, are soaked in these mustard oil com-
pounds, the caterpillars will munch away at them, just
as if they were cabbage leaves.

Smell also plays a part in caterpillar feeding. Both
the maxillae and the antennae have odor-sensitive cells,
with a total of about 40 on each side of the head.
Since these may vary in sensitivity to aromas, the
caterpillar is able to sense small differences among the
leaves it is exposed to. A caterpillar on a large plant
may never need this ability. But if it lives on such a
small plant that it eats up all the leaves, this fine sense
of smell would enable it to find its next meal with
ease.

Strange Diets

The vast majority of caterpillars feed on leaves or
other soft plant parts, such as flowers. Some young
lepidopterans, however, do have unusual diets. Car-
penter moth and leopard moth caterpillars (Cossidae)
bore into wood. They feed on various kinds of trees
and may seriously damage them. Because wood is a
food very low in nutritive value, these moths require
two or three years to complete their life cycles. Wax
moth larvae (one member of the large family Pyralidae) live within beehives and eat the beeswax which
makes up the comb. They can cause serious damage
to the hive.

Some caterpillars eat other animals rather than plants. In Florida there is a moth whose larvae feed on sucking insects called scale insects. Ants guard the scale insects and "milk" them for a sweet liquid they produce called honeydew. If the ants find a caterpillar eating scale insects they are guarding, they attack. The caterpillar swings around and dabs the ants with a fluid which it brings up from its stomach. The ants flee from the caterpillar, trying to clean the unpleasant stuff off their bodies as they go. This leaves the caterpillar free to continue feeding.

A few caterpillars actually stalk their prey. Those of one blue (Lycaenidae) from Africa play a trick on their victims. These caterpillars prey on other insects tended by ants, called jassids. A hungry caterpillar at first crawls slowly towards its prey, stopping often and vibrating its legs. When closer, it vibrates only the front legs, which apparently mimic the antennae of an attending ant. If its stalking is successful, the caterpillar ends up with its front legs vibrating right on top of the closed wings of its victim. Then it pounces, grabbing the jassid with all its legs and delivering a quick bite behind the head. The caterpillar takes a few quick mouthfuls and when its prey can no longer move, it relaxes, holding on with only its front legs while it polishes off its meal. These caterpillars have hard bodies covered with horny bumps and coarse hairs which probably help protect it from any ants guarding the jassids.

A peculiar geometrid moth larva has been discovered in Hawaii which feeds more like a praying mantis than a caterpillar. The claws on the first six legs of this caterpillar are long and have spines which can form a basketlike trap for catching flies. The caterpillar has to grab fast to capture flies, but it is an efficient hunter. Only four flies provide enough food to carry this unusual creature through to adulthood.

Living in Groups

While most lepidopterans lay their eggs singly, quite a few deposit them in groups. Often the larvae of these kinds stay together as they feed and grow and can cause considerable damage to their unfortunate plant hosts. Sometimes the colonial caterpillars are poisonous, and they can live fearlessly in the open once predators learn to leave them alone.

Group living has its advantages, too, to nonpoisonous caterpillars. Tent caterpillars are notoriously successful pests. The female moth lays a cluster of eggs on a twig. The eggs hatch out in the springtime, just as the leaves of the unfortunate tree are unfolding. The caterpillars spin out silken threads wherever they go. While they may wander off over the branches, the caterpillars tend to gather in one particular area. Because of all the silk laid down in this central place, a distinctive "tent" develops there. The tent is like a protected house. It acts like a greenhouse and stays warmer inside than it is outside. Even if the spring is

Almost everyone knows what the messy and destructive tent caterpillars look like; their adult form is an inconspicuous, very hairy moth with simple wing patterns.

cool and the temperature outside is cold enough to slow the caterpillars down, inside the tent their bodies can be warm enough to feed well.

As the insects grow, they leave the tent to feed with increasing frequency, returning to their shelter to rest. Within the warm tent they can digest their food more efficiently than out on the cooler branches. If the caterpillars are out feeding and sense a storm coming, they scurry back into the tent where they can stay warm and dry no matter how hard it pours. During their development, they may make several tents as they consume all the leaves within reach. Only when they are fully grown and ready to pupate do they leave the protected comfort of their tent for more than a short time. Then they leave it forever, looking for individual protected places to spin their cocoons.

Protection for Plants

Besides caterpillars, many other insects attack plants. If they had no way to fight back, plants would have lost out long ago. But despite the tremendous number of insects, the plants around us are healthy and thriving. There are many ways a plant can defend itself against being completely eaten up. The young leaves of many tropical forest trees are red. This may protect them from caterpillars, for most female butterflies are attracted to green when laying their eggs. Many plants have thorns which discourage insects from climbing onto them. Others, like holly, have waxy leaves with hard, sharp edges which are difficult for insects to attack. The leaves of other plants are covered by very small hairs. The hairs on one kind of passionflower vine have hooks which catch in the skin of butterfly caterpillars attempting to feed on the plant. The hooks puncture the skin, trapping the caterpillar and making wounds which may make it bleed to death.

A great many plants contain strong poisons which can sicken or kill animals which eat them. These plants, such as mustard and milkweed, are left alone by many plant-eaters. But some insects, including many lepidopterans, have turned the tables on poisonous plants. They have developed immunity to the poisons and even use them as cues for identifying food sources. Such insects tend to specialize on one group of poisonous plants. The whites feed on mustard family plants such as wild mustard or cabbage. Monarchs and queens eat various milkweeds, and passionflower butterflies attack poisonous passionflower vines. The caterpillars of such lepidopterans often get an extra bonus from their feeding habits. They store the poisons from the plants in their bodies and are thus themselves poisonous or distasteful to predators. As we will see later, usually this distastefulness is passed on to the adult butterfly or moth, too.

5 · The Great Change

When the caterpillar has grown to full size, its behavior changes. Instead of heading for the nearest leaf and munching away, it stops eating altogether and begins wandering. Some caterpillars merely travel until they locate a handy stem on their food plant, but others go longer distances. The sight of woolly bears marching across the road or up the side of a house is familiar. These caterpillars look for a high, sheltered spot before entering the pupal stage. The large green tomato hornworm wanders away from its host plant and burrows into the ground before shedding its last caterpillar skin.

The changes which turn a caterpillar into a moth or butterfly are so great that the insect is completely helpless and immobile while they are taking place. The pupa provides a hard covering inside of which the body of the caterpillar becomes reworked into the body of an adult lepidopteran.

The remodeling is considerable. The caterpillar

mouth, with its biting and chewing parts, must be totally rearranged. The strong, sharp mandibles disappear, while the small maxillae are drawn out to form the long, thin proboscis of the adult. The lower lip of the caterpillar has two small, smooth sensory organs called palps and provides an opening for the silk-producing spinnerets. In the adult, the palps are large and covered with scales and hairs, while the spinnerets are gone.

The fat, continuous body of the caterpillar becomes separated into a thorax and an abdomen. The first three pairs of legs are replaced by long thin adult legs, while the other five pairs completely disappear. Where no trace of wings was seen before, large, colorful wings grow, and the soft caterpillar cuticle becomes the much harder adult exoskeleton.

At first glance, the pupa may not look anything like a living insect. But if you examine it closely, you can see the outlines of the adult lepidopteran quite clearly. There are bumps where the compound eyes develop, and long ridges represent the antennae. Flattened plates on thé sides of the pupa outline the position of the wings. The abdomen, with its spiracles functioning all the time, is clearly visible.

Controlling the Changes

For thousands of years, humans viewed the change from caterpillar into butterfly as a magical transformation, and it has only been within the last 30 years or so that we have come to understand how the changes of metamorphosis are controlled by the lepidopteran body.

The secret of metamorphosis lies in substances produced by the body, called hormones. These are chemicals made in certain glands; they are circulated and affect the cells in particular ways. One hormone, called molting hormone or ecdysone, causes the caterpillar to shed its skin. Ecdysone is made by glands in the thorax. These glands are stimulated to produce or release ecdysone by another hormone from the brain, called brain hormone. During the caterpillar stage, the lepidopteran body is dominated by juvenile hormone. If the level of juvenile hormone in the body is high at the time of a molt, the caterpillar will molt into another caterpillar stage. When the larva molts into a pupa, there is less juvenile hormone present, while at the pupa-to-adult molt, juvenile hormone is absent.

These hormones can influence the behavior of the caterpillar as well as its body. When the insect ceases feeding and wanders about searching for a place to pupate, it is responding to the release into its body of a dose of molting hormone. If a caterpillar is experimentally injected with juvenile hormone before there would normally be a release of molting hormone, it molts again into a caterpillar instead of a pupa and does not stop feeding or look for a place to pupate.

The behavior of some lepidopterans is quite closely

regulated by the concentrations of hormones. The wax moth caterpillar spins a cocoon before each molt. During the larval stage this cocoon is long and open at both ends. But before the pupal molt, the cocoon is short, strong, and closed at both ends. Before molting, the full-grown caterpillar tears a hole in one end, leaving a flap through which the moth can exit. If the caterpillar is given juvenile hormone before it is supposed to molt into a pupa, it spins a different cocoon. It spins a typical caterpillar-type cocoon and then will molt into another caterpillar stage. But if the juvenile hormone is not completely effective in keeping it a larva, it spins an intermediate sort of cocoon and molts into a creature somewhere between a larva and a pupa in body structure.

Becoming a Pupa

Different caterpillars behave differently before changing into pupae. Some moth caterpillars burrow into the ground and simply molt into a shiny brown pupa. Others spin a thick silken cocoon inside of which they molt into protected pupae. The caterpillar may pull the edges of a leaf together to enclose its cocoon, or it may suspend itself on a long silken thread hanging from a tree. Some butterfly caterpillars also spin simple cocoons. Most butterfly larvae spin a silk pad which they grab with special hooks on the tip of the abdomen. Some simply hang head downward from

This promethea moth caterpillar has spun a thick silk cocoon which is protected by a leaf it has characteristically folded inward over it. These cocoons are easy to see during the winter and can be collected to observe the adults emerging in the spring; they should be kept in covered containers (with air holes) in a cool or cold place till spring to prevent their emerging too early.

this pad, while others also spin a supporting girdle of silk which attaches to the midsection of the body.

After securing itself, the caterpillar begins to shed its skin. Waves of muscle contraction split the dull old caterpillar skin, and the very different pupal skin is unveiled bit by bit. The old skin is pushed toward the rear end where it forms a crumpled mass. The pupa must next perform a tricky but vital maneuver. It must release the hooks, flip away the larval skin, and grab its silk pad again without falling. Although this looks like a formidable task, few fail. Now the pupa becomes quiet, capable of only the slightest twitching movements, until the butterfly is ready to emerge.

During the pupal stage, the lepidopteran is quite helpless. A firmly anchored pupa may be hard for a predator to rip away from its mooring, but the pupa cannot escape if it is discovered. It is not surprising, then, that most pupae are green or brown in color, or camouflaged in some other way. The green pupae of many butterflies have beautiful shining golden flecks which look like drops of dew or bits of light shining through the leaves. It is these bits of gold that give the butterfly pupa its name, chrysalis, from *chrysos*, the Greek word for "gold." There are pupae which resemble twigs, leaves, flower buds, even pebbles or bird droppings. Some have horns or spines which help further in their camouflage. The cuticle of the pupa is very hard, too, which may discourage possible predators.

Becoming a Butterfly

While the outside of the pupa looks quiet, inside there is great activity. Actually, the changes from caterpillar to adult begin before the pupa is even formed. The clusters of adult cells in the caterpillar's body have been kept inactive by juvenile hormone. When the level of juvenile hormone begins to drop in the mature caterpillar, these cells "wake up." They begin growing and dividing rapidly, starting to organize into parts of the butterfly or moth. Thus, inside the wandering caterpillar, the adult is already forming. By the time the caterpillar molts into the pupa, the adult is already well on its way.

The wings begin to form when the caterpillar is fully grown. Under the larval skin the wing cells multi-

How lepidopteran wings form, as shown in a cross-section of the thorax. In 1, cells of the inner skin grow inward (arrows) to form pockets where wing buds will develop. In 2, cells grow outward into the pockets to form wing buds, and the tracheae begin sending out branches. Number 3 shows the growing wings with their tracheae. By stage 4, the wings have been pushed out of their pockets and grow down the sides of the body, still inside the caterpillar cuticle. In 5, the caterpillar cuticle has been shed, and the forming pupal cuticle is indicated by the dashed line. Stage 6 shows the wing development after the pupa is formed, with wings almost meeting under the body, their shape now outlined by the pupal cuticle. Drawing by the author.

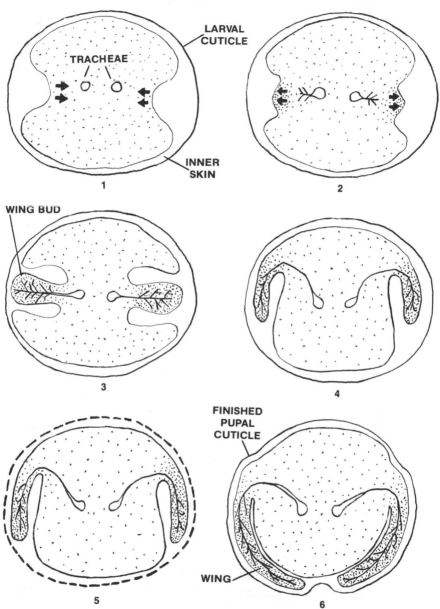

ply, pushing inward to form pockets at the sides of the body. Then the wing buds grow outward, filling the cavities of the pockets. As the wings grow, branches of the tracheae grow into them. The top and bottom of the wing bud will form the upper and lower wing membranes, while the branches of the tracheal system will form the wing veins, sandwiched between the two membranes.

After the caterpillar has spun its silken pad and attached itself, the wing buds push out of their pockets and grow down along the sides of the caterpillar's body, still beneath the last larval skin so that they cannot be seen. Just before the caterpillar sheds, these wing buds sometimes become visible. Between the time the larva sheds and the pupal case hardens, the wings grow very rapidly and spread until they are almost touching under the thorax of the pupa. During this period, the wings increase to eight times the size they were when the skin was shed.

Inside the pupa, the larval structures are being broken down at the same time that the adults parts are forming. Blood cells called phagocytes, which are like amebas, engulf bits of the degenerating larval organs. The larval cells die, releasing the energy they have stored up for use in constructing the adult body. The adult organs grow rapidly with the abundant supply of fuel. While the larva is being dismantled, the contents of the pupa are largely fluid. But bit by bit, the winged adult is forming. The circles of simple eyes are transformed into the huge compound eyes of the adult. The muscular system is completely rearranged. The muscles needed for the body contractions and simple stepping of the caterpillar are very different from those required for flapping wings and the distinct walking movements of long, jointed legs. The reproductive system, barely represented in the caterpillar, matures so that the butterfly can carry out its function of reproduction. Some parts of the larva change little during metamorphosis. The heart, tracheae, and nervous system remain basically the same.

While the changes from caterpillar to butterfly or moth are very great, they can occur amazingly fast. Some butterflies and moths crawl out of their pupae only a few days after shedding the last caterpillar skin. Others may remain as pupae for months or even years. Quite a few lepidopterans spend the winter or dry season as pupae and emerge as adults when the weather warms up or the rains come.

Taking Wing

Coming out of the pupa is a fairly easy matter for a butterfly with a chrysalis on a twig. But a buried pupa must wriggle to the surface so the moth can crawl out of the soil. Pupae inside sturdy cocoons may secrete a fluid which softens the silk threads so the moth can escape. Some silkworms leave a weak spot at one end of the cocoon where they do not glue the

A male polyphemus moth about three minutes after escaping from its pupa case. Lepidopterans vary a great deal, according to species, in the time it takes a caterpillar to become an adult.

threads together. Instead, they weave a cone with the small end pointing outward. The moth can wriggle out, separating the strands of the cocoon to enlarge the hole. But an enemy cannot enter the little hole from the outside while the pupa is helpless.

When the adult is about to emerge from the pupa, it changes in appearance. The colors of the wings can be seen through the pupal cuticle. The pupa splits behind the head and the butterfly first frees its legs and antennae. After a short rest it crawls out. It looks little like a butterfly, for the wings are soft, wet, and crumpled. It pumps blood into spaces around the tracheal veins, expanding the wings by stretching out the many minute folds which kept them compact within the pupa. Then the full beauty of the insect becomes evident, its colorful scales shining and perfect. Once the wings have hardened, the butterfly can fly off to live its new life floating on the breeze.

6 · On the Wing

The freedom of flight gives the adult lepidopteran a completely different life from that of its crawling larva, so it is no surprise to see its senses completely rearranged. The caterpillar has poor vision, its two circles of simple eyes probably able to see little more than light and shadow, or perhaps to make out the vertical line of a plant stem. The butterfly has huge eyes, bulging globes made up of as many as 36,000 individual tiny units, each with its own input to the brain. With these eyes, a butterfly can see in all directions around it except directly underneath its body.

It can see colors as well, including the ultraviolet rays which are invisible to our eyes. Only some butterflies can see red. Color of course is very important in their lives. They must be able to recognize the colors of the flowers they feed from and the green of leaves where they lay their eggs. Color also plays a role in the courtship and mating of some lepidopterans. Despite more than 150 years of study, we still are not certain just what sort of image the insect brain receives from the complicated compound eyes. We do not know if the signals from all the individual units are received separately so that a huge mosaic is perceived or if the signals are somehow combined to produce one large panorama. We cannot be sure just how sharp the image is, or how far away distinct shapes can be perceived.

Elegant Antennae

The caterpillar's antennae are short and fat. It need perceive only short-range odors. But adult butterflies and moths use their long, elegant antennae constantly, for the sense of smell is vital to their existence. They are attracted by the perfumes of the flowers they visit and, as we have already seen, odor is vital in the courtship of most lepidopterans. The long antennae are studded with thousands of odor-sensitive receptors called sensilla. These come in a bewildering array of sizes and shapes. Some are merely small round pits while others are tiny tapered spines. Some are very complicated, with a circle of minute spines surrounding a central peg.

Just why there are so many different kinds of sensilla is not understood, but it seems that their shapes must have some importance to the life of the insect. For example, the corn earworm moth has antennae with 90 segments each. Each segment is the same and

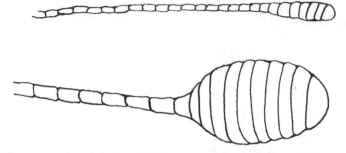

The antennae of butterflies are club-shaped, ending in a widened tip; such a shape occurs only rarely in moths.

has ten different kinds of sensilla. On one segment there may be over a hundred sensilla of one type, while others are less abundant. In some cases, such as the sensilla of the male silkworm moth which are sensitive to the female sex attractant, scientists have been able to determine that a particular type of sensillum is sensitive to a certain chemical in the air. But with so many kinds of sensilla and so many kinds of insects, it would be a hopeless task to try to identify individually the sensitivities of all types of sensilla in even a few different insect species.

The antennae are not used to sense only odors. They are also sensitive to touch and to vibrations. Some of the sensilla, then, are used for these senses. Butterflies lack ears, but the vibration sensitivity of their antennae may enable them to "hear" some sounds in a crude way. Most moths, too, lack ears. But a few kinds have special organs, on the thorax in some and on the abdomen in others, which enable them to hear the ultrasonic cries of their bat predators. (Even the pupal forms of some moths will respond with a twitch if a whistle is blown near them.) The bat uses the echoes bouncing back from objects as a way of navigating in the dark and of finding food. If a moth hears a bat's cry, it may react in one of several ways. If the bat is far off, the moth will fly fast and straight in the opposite direction. But if the bat is near, the moth may dive down suddenly or fly upward rapidly. Its behavior when a bat is nearby is quite unpredictable. This is an advantage to the moth, for if a predator cannot predict what sort of evasive action it will take, it has a better chance of escaping.

Tasting and Feeding

We have already seen that a female butterfly uses taste receptors on her feet to detect the chemical composition of leaves where she may lay her eggs. Sometimes it is difficult to separate the sense of smell from the sense of taste. Much of what we humans attribute to the taste of food is actually its smell. This is why food may "taste" flat if one has a head cold. A favorite stunt to show how much smell influences our sense of taste is to ask a blindfolded person to hold his nose and bite into a raw potato and an apple, trying to tell which is which. Under these circumstances it is almost impossible to distinguish the two foods.

Different receptors are used for taste and smell. Odor receptors are those which can detect chemicals in the air, while taste receptors detect them when dissolved in a fluid. The odor of something can be detected from a distance, for the distinctive chemicals can be carried by the air. But taste requires actual contact with the substance tasted.

The taste receptors on butterflies' feet are very important in feeding as well as in egg-laying. When a butterfly's feet come in contact with a sweet solution, its long, coiled proboscis automatically unrolls. Some butterflies are extremely sensitive to sugar. A monarch will respond when its feet touch a sugar solution with only one part of sugar for 120,400 parts of water. Its feet are more than 2000 times as sensitive as the human tongue.

The proboscis is a complicated organ. It is formed by two long tubes, one on the right side and one on the left. The inside edges of both tubes are concave (rounded inwardly), so that there is a third tube formed between them. The two halves are held together by minute hooks. The central tube is used for sucking up nectar or other food. The two side channels are spaces into which blood can flow.

When the insect feeds, blood enters the side channels, forcing the proboscis to straighten out. When the proboscis is not being used in feeding, the blood returns to the body and the proboscis coils up again. The coil is maintained largely because of the elastic nature of the proboscis and possibly by muscle contraction as well. The lepidopteran has a muscular pump inside the throat which pulls food up through

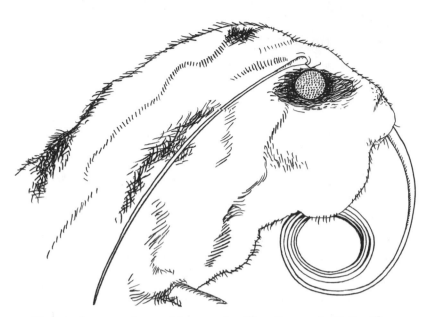

The proboscis of a sphinx moth, like those of all lepidopterans, is a very remarkable bodily "tool."

the proboscis. A bend in its middle enables the butterfly to insert it into curved flowers. There are taste receptors on its tip, and if you watch closely, you may see a butterfly probing here and there in a flower to taste it before settling down to suck the nectar.

Lepidopteran Foods

While the caterpillar stores up food energy used by the adult insect, many butterflies and moths do gain significant energy from feedings as adults. Nectar is the most common food. Butterflies visit only certain kinds of flowers, and certain butterflies may favor particular flowers. Any blossom which feeds the insects must have a place for them to land. For this reason, butterflies like flowers that grow in clusters or which have a strong, wide lower petal. Some butterflies, such as whites and swallowtails, can see red and feed from flowers such as pinks. Butterfly flowers have the nectar hidden inside of long tubes where most insects cannot reach it.

Sphinxes and hawkmoths also feed on nectar. They fly at night and can hover in front of a flower while feeding. The blossoms they frequent tend to be white or greenish in color and so can be seen in the dark, and they do not have landing places. Unlike bees, most nectar-feeding butterflies and moths do not feed on pollen and must receive all their nourishment from the nectar. Flowers which attract butterflies have a fairly high content of amino acids, the chemicals used in making body proteins.

Especially in the tropics, many butterflies have other foods instead of or in addition to nectar. Some feed at puddles of urine, while others suck at rotten fruit. Some visit decaying bodies, while others frequent bird droppings. The long-lived Heliconius butterflies (Heliconidae) feed on pollen. There are small projections on the tip of the proboscis which the butterfly uses to scrape up pollen.

Moths, too, have a variety of food sources. While many moths do not feed at all, others live a long time and need abundant food resources. The long, delicate proboscis of most lepidopterans is not suited for much

Some butterflies take in certain fluids besides nectar. These tiger swallowtails (Papilio glaucus) are "puddling," or sucking in water containing naturally occurring salts. Salt is a necessity for virtually all animals.

more than sucking up liquid food. But some moths have developed a stronger, piercing proboscis which can penetrate fruits. Some can feed only on soft berries, while others have a proboscis strong enough to plunge through the thick skin of oranges. One such moth is so successful at this task that it has become a significant orchard pest.

Feeding from Mammals

A few moths have turned away from plant-feeding and head for the bodies of warm-bloodied animals when they are hungry. Certain species from two families (Geometridae and Pyralidae) have such habits. They search out pockets of sweat, oil, or blood on the hides of large mammals. Other moths (in the family Noctuidae) have the nasty habit of concentrating on mammalian eyes, sucking at eye discharges or tears. Fortunately, such moths are found only in the tropics. Sometimes they even attack human eyes, although they usually prey on such animals as pigs, elephants, buffaloes, antelopes, and deer.

A few moths have even evolved the ability to feed on blood. They lick up blood from wounds in the body or from excess blood excreted by engorged mosquitos. One kind is actually able to pierce the tough hide of mammals and suck blood like a mosquito. This moth has a short, strong proboscis with sharp spines which aid in penetrating the skin. When attacking, the moth

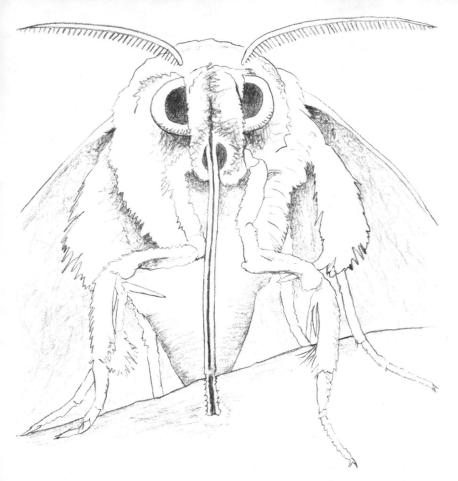

This is the Malayan moth Calpe eustrigata, *the one species of moth known that has evolved into a skin-piercing, blood-sucking lepidopteran. It has put its rather complicated two-part proboscis through human skin and is "sawing" its way deeper to find a good blood supply.*

first bends its proboscis to one side and then the other, poking with the sharp tips of the two proboscis halves in turn. As it does this, the proboscis vibrates like a miniature jack-hammer, poking the skin relentlessly with about 35 jabs each second.

Once the skin is penetrated, the minute hooks around the proboscis tip quickly rip open a wound big enough for the proboscis to enter. Then the moth drives in its spiny weapon by alternately poking with the right and left halves of the proboscis, which can slide past each other. Backward-pointing spines catch in the flesh and keep the proboscis from pulling out. Once it hits a blood vessel, the moth can suck its fill. The proboscis spines are movable. When the moth is through feeding, it relaxes the spines so that they point downward, and the proboscis can be pulled out with ease.

Flying Jewels

Their large, often exquisitely beautiful scaled wings set lepidopterans apart from all other insects. Scales are a major reason for the success and diversity of these creatures. Not only can the scales take on every color of the rainbow, they aid flying ability as well. Scales improve lepidopteran gliding and increase the lifting ability of the wings by about 15 per cent. They also provide a protective covering for the delicate wing membranes and help strengthen the wings with their minute ridges and their overlapping arrangement.

There are two basic types of wing colors. Most colors are due to actual pigments within the scales and sometimes the wing membranes themselves. Black, brown, red, and reddish-brown colors are produced by pigments. The white, yellow, orange, and red shades typical of whites and sulphurs are derived from pigments found only in this butterfly family. In other butterflies, cream and yellow colors may come from chemicals taken in by the caterpillar from its food plant and passed directly on to the adult.

The brilliant green, blue, silver, and gold colors especially common in tropical butterflies are not caused by pigments. Instead, they are the result of light reflection from minute ridges on the scales—what a physicist calls diffraction. The ridges and layers of such scales can be incredibly detailed. The swallowtail butterfly *Papilio ulyssus* is one of the most brilliant blue butterflies in all the world. This five-inch beauty lives in a large area through the forests of the East Indies into northern Australia. Since it inhabits the treetops it is not frequently seen, but it can be lured down near the ground with scraps of blue cloth. This attraction to blue hints that their brilliant colors are important in some way to the reproductive behavior of these forest fliers. The surface of each wing scale of this butterfly has tiny ridges about 1/1000 millimeter apart. Blue light has a short wavelength and is reflected from the scales, while colors of longer wavelength are absorbed by them. The scale surface has coarse ridges, too, which allow the blue color to be seen from many different angles.

The morphos of tropical America also live in the forest treetops and have iridescent blue (or green) colors. One sometimes sees jewelry made from bits of their beautiful wings. Morpho colors change, depending on the angle from which one looks. Their scales are even more complicated than those of *Papilio ulyssus*. One species from Rio de Janeiro has brilliant blue wings which take on different shades when viewed from various angles. Its scales have a series of tiny ridges between 1050 and 1400 millimeters apart. The sides of each of these are further sculptured into layers of clear, parallel platforms. The distance between the platforms is such that all wavelengths are trapped except blue. When the wings are viewed from different angles, the distance between platforms seems to change, resulting in the changes in color. Each scale has a slightly curved surface, too, so that the iridescence is visible from all angles. Black pigment under the sculpturing also helps absorb all the other light wavelengths.

Sometimes the iridescent scales are mixed with pigmented ones and produce exquisite color combinations. Some scales have both pigment and sculpturing, producing striking color combinations or unexpected changes. The Formosa birdwing has black forewings. The hindwings are a rich golden yellow when viewed from above, but shift to an intriguing mixture of iridescent blue, green, and pink if viewed at an angle from behind.

Quite a few lepidopterans have completely clear areas on their wings. These may be small "windows" as on the wings of some woodland butterflies and large moths, or they may involve practically the whole wing, as in many forest-dwelling ithomiids. In these butterflies, the scales are reduced to very fine, colorless hairs.

Wing Veins

Lepidopteran wings are marked by often dark, branching veins. The veins are interesting to scientists who classify and name butterflies and moths, for their patterns can reveal something about the relationships of a new species. But to most people, the wing veins are much more interesting in the functions they serve to their bearers.

The veins help support the wings. There are two especially strong veins along the front edges of the forewings which help keep the beating wings stiff. But the veins have other functions, too. Each vein is really a tube within a tube. The inside tube is a branch of the tracheal system and is filled with air. The outer, surrounding tube is filled with blood. When the lepidopteran crawls out of its pupa into the light, blood is pumped into these veins, forcing the wings to expand and unfold fully. After the wings have hardened, most of the blood returns to the body. But a leisurely bit of circulation is maintained in the wing veins and is vital to the survival of some butterflies, at least in colder climates.

Solar Heating

Butterflies can often be seen basking in the sun while perched on flowers. They hold their wings out, tipped toward the sun. The butterfly body must reach a minimum temperature before it can fly, and so it basks. The wing veins in many cases are black. The black pigment absorbs heat from the sun which is passed into the body by the blood circulating in the veins.

Butterflies in northern areas often have darker wings than their more southerly cousins. They tend to fly close to the ground where it is warmer from the sun's reflected heat. Some kinds have the dark pigment on their upper wings. The walls of the veins are thinner on the top surface than on the bottom, too, and so can more easily absorb the sun's heat. Such butterflies bask facing away from the sun, with their bodies raised so that their open wings are maximally exposed to the rays. If the sun passes behind a cloud, the butterflies may quickly snap their wings closed rather than lose any of the precious heat back to the cool air.

Northern sulphurs and whites, on the other hand, have darker wing undersides, especially on the hindwings, than do southern kinds. When their body temperature is below about 35° C. (95° F.), these butterflies bask with their wings closed and tip their bodies

When butterflies vary their positions and change their wing angles, these may seem to us just casual and meaningless movements. However, they are often adjustments to get warmer or cooler, depending on the sun's angle and intensity.

so that the dark underwing is perpendicular to the sun. This gives the maximum area for absorbing heat. In this position, the butterfly's thorax and abdomen lie right under the darkest part of the wing, so that the body can absorb heat directly through the wings.

Butterflies must avoid overheating, too. When it is warm and a sulfur's body reaches about 38° C. (100° F.), it rests with its closed wings parallel to the sun's rays. In this position, its wings absorb almost no heat at all. The lighter colors of more southerly butterflies keep them from warming up too quickly. And during the heat of the day, butterflies can always retreat to shady places to await the cooler evening.

7 · Avoiding Enemies

Beautiful butterfly colors may please our eyes and be useful to some species during their courtship and mating. Dark colors may also function in regulating the body temperature of these "cold-blooded" creatures. But most of the variety of lepidopteran colors and patterns exist for none of these reasons. They are there because of the effect they have on hungry enemies of lepidopterans, especially birds. Birds have very keen eyesight and good color vision. They are capable of learning from experience and have surprisingly long memories. All these attributes of birds affect in one way or another the ways butterfly and moth wing patterns protect them from their biggest enemies.

A bird can hardly eat an insect it cannot see. A tremendous number of lepidopterans have amazingly detailed camouflaging patterns. Many moth species spend the daytime resting on tree trunks, their mottled brown wings blending in perfectly with the bark. Some small moths can roll up their wings when they rest and thus look like dead leaves. Other wing-rollers settle on trees and rest with their bodies pointing up at an angle, resembling dead twigs.

Moths may disguise their shapes in more drastic ways. One sphinx moth in West Africa rests with its leaf-patterned, brown wings raised above its brown abdomen. The edges of the wings curl, making the whole moth resemble a torn, dried-up leaf. An unrelated Brazilan moth contorts its body more drastically. Hanging on the end of a dead vine, it bends its brown-patterned wings downward instead of up. Each wing is slightly curved. Their shape and pattern combine with the insect's fat abdomen, which is bent a full 180° over its head, to create a very unmothlike impression of a dead and faded flower.

Many butterflies have inconspicuous brown colors which help them "disappear" when they land. The most nearly perfect butterfly disguise is that of the Asian leaf butterflies. Their wings are held together at rest and look exactly like dried, dead leaves. There are even "tails" on the hindwings which become the leaf stalk when the butterfly alights. Wing markings mimic the veins of a leaf, and even spots of mold or other imperfections such as worm holes are suggested.

The anglewings, such as the question mark and comma butterflies, are common American leaf mimics. The rough margin of the outer wing edges combines with the mottled brown underwing markings to make a fine dead leaf. These butterflies pass the winter as

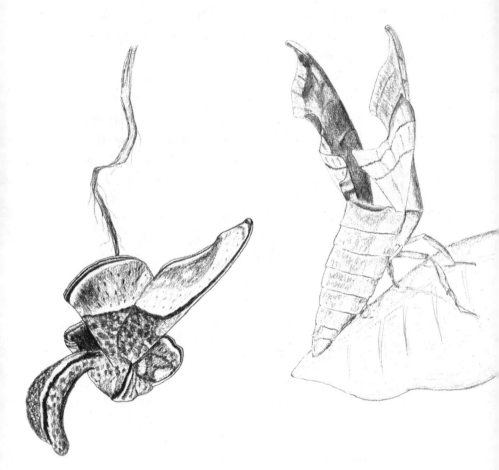

Camouflage occurs in many insect groups, including lepidopterans. At left is a moth on the end of a jungle vine, twisting its body till it resembles a dead flower. It can remain for hours in this unlikely position. The African sphinx moth on the right holds its head down and its wings up, resembling a dried, curled leaf. Drawing by the author.

adults, mixed in with leaves in trash heaps and hollow trees. Their camouflage is vital for their survival while they are helpless and birds are hungry.

Sometimes colors which look bright and conspicuous when seen away from the butterfly's natural habitat turn out to be disguising in natural surroundings. A tiger swallowtail, with its bright yellow, black-striped wings, stands out when fluttering across a meadow. But in the dappled sun and shade of the trees, the light and dark of the butterfly's wings help it blend in well. Orange and brown patterns are common in butterflies. These look colorful pinned in an insect box, but break up the butterfly shape in the blotches of light and dark near the forest floor. Some wildly patterned butterflies are disguised by the confusion of their designs. The zebra butterfly (Colobura) of tropical America has zigs and zags of brown and cream which completely disguise the shape of its wings. A bird wouldn't even recognize it as a butterfly, for the confusion of markings makes it almost impossible to discern the typical wing outline.

Eyespots

A great many butterflies and moths have wing markings which look like eyes. There may be a row of small markings along the edge of the wing or a pair or two of large ones. Scientists have debated the function of these common markings. Since they are

Many butterflies and moths, like this polyphemus moth, have "eyes" on their wings that very probably frighten away birds and other predators.

found in so many different, unrelated lepidopterans, they must be important in their lives. The usual explanation for the small wing-edge spots is that they distract bird predators into pecking at the wings instead of at the more vulnerable body of the insect. A butterfly or moth can lose a piece of wing and be little the worse for wear. But if a bird pecks its body, it can be seriously wounded.

The larger eyespots may well frighten birds away altogether. A scientist named Dr. David Blest studied the reactions of birds to eyespot patterns. He found that some were startled by a pair of simple round spots, but most were positively frightened by eyelike designs. He also studied bird reactions to the peacock

butterfly. The underwings of this insect are camouflaged by leaflike patterns. But if it is disturbed, the
peacock opens its wings with a hissing sound, revealing its four large, prominent eyespots. While birds
acted afraid of normal peacock butterflies, they were
rarely startled by ones whose scales (and therefore
eyespot patterns) had been rubbed off. Blest's studies
provide pretty solid evidence that eyespot patterns can
frighten predators away.

The eyed hawkmoth has its eyespots on the upper
sides of the hindwings only. The moth rests on tree
trunks with the front wings covering the hindwings.
If disturbed, it pulls the forewings forward, revealing
the big eyespots. It also moves its body up and down,

*Caterpillars too can have eyespots that appear to protect
them against would-be predators. This spicebush swallowtail
larva actually has nothing in the way of eyes except the usual
very small and weak ocelli at the front of the head (at right).*
                                                    ALICE L. HOPF

adding to the illusion. This display may fool predators into thinking that a big owl has appeared suddenly in a tree hole.

Many hairstreaks and blues (Lycaenidae) have a complete false-head design. An eyespot on each hindwing combines with a pair of "tails" which resemble antennae. The butterfly may even gently move the wings, increasing the illusion that the head is really at the back end of the insect. Some tropical species have two or even three pairs of these tails, with one pair even longer than the body. Possibly the extra pairs are taken for legs, increasing the bodylike look of the wings.

Other lepidopterans have what can be called "startle displays" which do not involve eyespots. The underwing moths (members of the large family Noctuidae) have camouflaging patterns on their forewings which disguise them against tree trunks. But if disturbed, these common lepidopterans raise their forewings to reveal bright red or pink hindwings. Presumably the startled hesitation of a predator confronted with the sudden, bright hindwing display would give the moth just enough time to escape before its enemy recovered from its surprise.

"Copying" Other Animals

When an insect fools predators by its appearance, the deception is not conscious. The insect has no

awareness of its disguise. Its shape and color patterns
have evolved to their present state because, over many
generations, individuals with the deceptive designs,
and behavior that matches them effectively, have
survived long enough to reproduce and pass on
their traits to their offspring, whereas more conspicuous species often die young and leave few offspring.
The amazing forms and patterns which exist today in
many insect groups are the result of thousands of
generations of insects' gradually evolving better and
better ways to "fool" the sharp eyes of predators.

Harmless moths may be protected by their resemblance to dangerous or poisonous insects or spiders.
One moth has striking tan and white markings on its
wings and hairy legs and body. The markings help
disguise its wings. The moth holds its first pair of legs
out in front and carries the other two out to the sides,
giving it an alarming resemblance to a dangerous
tarantula spider.

Several moths have bands of yellow or orange,
giving them a wasplike look. If one of these moths is
disturbed, it lifts its abdomen and makes movements
suggesting it is about to sting. Another moth has shiny
black wings like many wasps. It has yellow bands on
the underside of its abdomen and a bright orange
mock sting which it waves at potential enemies.

Most hawkmoths fly by night. But a few kinds go
about in bright daylight. You may even have seen
one without recognizing it as a moth, for these clear-

wing hawkmoths look almost exactly like bumblebees. Their wings are practically scaleless and are clear except for the brown edges and veins. Their bodies are fuzzy-looking and banded in black and yellow, with different species resembling various kinds of bumblebees.

One entire family of moths, the clearwings (Aegeriidae or Sessiidae) consists of mimics of wasps and bees. Their bodies are thin and smooth with bands of black, yellow, orange, or red. Some resemble bumblebees, while others look like tiny, delicate parasitic wasps. These moths are fast daytime fliers whose disguise apparently protects them well from predators.

"Copying" One Another

We have already seen that quite a few lepidopterans are poisonous. This quality is generally accompanied by a bad taste and may make a bird violently ill. Any bird which experiences this kind of discomfort is likely to remember it and associate it with the offending insect. Poisonous or distasteful lepidopterans usually have bright colors, often with simple patterns; a bright, simple pattern should be easy to remember. The orange monarch with its black wing veins and edges is a fine example. And what about the viceroy butterfly, which looks so much like the monarch? It turns out that the viceroy is completely edible and makes a fine bit of bird feed. But if a bird has had a bad experience with a bitter, poisonous monarch, it would hardly risk attacking another, almost identical orange butterfly.

This tendency of birds, and presumably other predators, to remember their bad experiences and avoid the causes of these experiences had led to an incredible variety of butterflies and moths, as well as other insects which mimic poisonous species. Examples of this sort of mimicry can be found around the world. The pipevine swallowtail, common in the southern states but also found farther north, feeds on poisonous plants as a caterpillar. The adult butterfly is poisonous, too. Its upper wings are blackish blue, while the hindwing undersides have a crescent of bright orange spots over iridescent blue scales. Several other butterflies found in the same areas as the pipevine swallowtail are thought to be mimics; the spicebush swallowtail, the red-spotted purple, the Diana fritillary, and dark-colored females of two other swallowtails.

Another kind of mimicry is even more common in the tropics. Several species of poisonous lepidopterans, often including both butterflies and moths, or even beetles, may closely resemble one another. In this way, all species can benefit from the experience of predators with any species in the group, not just with others of its own kind. In some tropical areas, a dozen different species from three or four different butterfly families may look so much alike on the wing that a collector must net them and examine them closely to be sure just which species are involved.

Different Patterns

We may think that all individuals of a particular species should look pretty much alike, except for differences between the sexes. But this is not necessarily the case, for a variety of reasons. Some butterfly mimics which themselves are perfectly edible may have variable color patterns. Some individuals may mimic one poisonous species while others look like a different distasteful kind. The best known example of such a butterfly is the African mocker swallowtail. While all African mocker males look alike, the females come in a great variety of forms, many of which lack the typical "tails" of their hindwings completely. Many of these females look like one or another inedible butterfly, such as the African queen.

When animals of the same species exist in more than one form, like the African mocker, they are said to be polymorphic (which in Greek means "many forms"). This kind of polymorphism, in which some individuals mimic one poisonous species and others resemble another, can be explained by thinking about predator behavior. If there are lots of poisonous butterflies with a particular pattern and only a few edible ones, the chances are that a predator will experience an inedible butterfly first and avoid the color pattern from then on. But if there are many tasty individuals with a particular pattern, there is a pretty good chance that the predator will attack an edible one first and keep eating butterflies with that pattern until it encounters a distasteful one.

For this reason there cannot be too many mimics or they will lose a significant amount of protection. This severely limits the possible population of mimic species. But if the butterflies mimic several inedible kinds, the mimic species can have a large population. While the number of butterflies with any particular pattern may be low, the total of individuals in the species can be high without being endangered.

More Color Variations

Not all the varieties of the African mocker resemble inedible butterflies, however, and other kinds of butterflies and moths may be highly variable without being mimics. The Malayan leaf butterfly has a great variety of different forms which are various combinations of eight or ten different patterns. Many species of underwing moths, too, show considerable variation in their forewing designs. Again, the probable explanation for such variations lies in bird behavior.

When birds hunt, they do not randomly look for anything that might be tasty. If a bird finds a moth, say, which was edible, it is likely next to look for other identical moths. This is called using a "searching image," and probably increases the likelihood of hunting success. Bees use the same sort of behavior when hunting for food; they tend to stick with one sort of flower. Humans do it, too. If you are looking for a particular book which you know has a red cover, you will concentrate on looking for red covers, rapidly scanning the books around and looking closely only at those with red covers.

Scientists believe that lepidopterans with variable color patterns are getting around the searching image of birds. If there are several different-looking forms, only one form will be discovered by the hungry bird and others can avoid being eaten. This sort of variability in pattern would be especially important for camouflaged species which rely on their "invisibility" as their main predator defense. The fact that such variation is common in camouflaged species, such as underwing moths, leaf butterflies, and anglewings, is evidence in support of this idea.

Changing with the Seasons

Butterfly species which produce more than one generation each year may have different color patterns at different seasons. Sometimes the differences are so great that it is hard to believe the two forms belong to the same species. The European map butterfly has brown and orange wings in spring and blackish-brown wings with small white bands in summer. The African commodore is bright orange with some black markings during the wet season, while dry-season individuals have dark black and blue wings with only a few orange spots. Wing shape may also vary with the seasons, with more irregular edges on wings of dry-season butterflies than on those of wet-season forms.

The reasons for this type of variation are not clear, especially in temperate-zone butterflies with differing spring and summer forms. It seems that the dry season butterflies are more camouflaged in color pattern than wet-season ones. Since they may remain inactive for part of the season, these butterflies could benefit from camouflage. Since dry-season forms have more irregular and leaflike wing edges, small or nonexistent eyespots, and more variable patterns which could escape the searching images of birds, camouflage appears to be a reasonable explanation for the dry-season patterns.

Butterfly pupae often vary in color with the seasons, too. Butterflies with two or more generations a year may pass the winter as pupae. A green pupa is camouflaged in summer whereas a brown one is inconspicuous during the winter. Scientists studied a swallowtail with green summer and brown winter pupae. They found that a larva growing up when days were short produced a brown pupa. One growing up under long days, however, could molt into either a brown or a green pupa, depending on the color of the material it rested on to pupate. If it chose a brown background such as a tree trunk, its pupa was brown. If a green leaf or stem was selected, the resulting pupa was green. The difference in pupal color is regulated by a

hormone which may be released just before the caterpillar pupates. If the hormone is released, the pupa
is brown. If no hormone is circulated, the pupa is
green.

Caterpillar Camouflage

Caterpillars are even more defenseless than adult
lepidopterans. Their mouths are not adapted to biting
enemies and they have no stings. Unlike their parents,
they cannot escape their enemies by flying away. For
these reasons, caterpillars are often protectively colored. A green caterpillar resting on the underside of
a leaf, such as a cabbage "worm," is likely to go unnoticed both by birds which hunt in the garden and
by gardeners searching for pests. If you look closely,
you can see that many green caterpillars are not evenly
colored. The green along their backs may be darker
than along their undersides. This effect is called countershading and is found in many animals. The lighter
underside becomes darkened by the shadow of the
body. If it were the same color as the top side, it would
look darker because of the shadow, and the caterpillar
would stand out instead of blending in. Caterpillars
which rest upside down, such as those of some hawkmoths and silkmoths, have reverse countershading.
Their backs are lighter than their undersides.

Caterpillars have other structures and markings
which help them melt into the background. Under-

wing moth caterpillars have tiny fringes along their bodies which help break up the outline of their bodies and make them blur into the leaves or twigs on which they rest. The appearance and behavior of these caterpillars may change as they grow, disguising them differently as they increase in size. A newly hatched underwing caterpillar is often translucent, and the green color of the leaf shows right through its body. This little larva rests along the outer edge of the leaf, where its small size makes it barely noticeable. When it is larger, its color darkens and it lies in a straight line right along the leaf rib. The still larger, later caterpillar rests along the "stem" of the leaf (called the petiole) where it again blends in perfectly. Then, when it molts for the third time, it loses its green color and has a more barklike appearance. It also moves off the leaves when not feeding and rests on twigs, moving to larger and larger twigs as it grows.

Many of us are familiar with inchworms. These are caterpillars of one of the largest moth families, the Geometridae. Instead of having four pairs of prolegs near the middle of the body and a fifth pair near the rear end, these caterpillars have no prolegs near the middle and two or three pairs near the rear. They move by looping the body forward, placing the rear end behind the front and then stretching out the front to a new foothold. Many inchworms look remarkably like twigs. If disturbed, they merely stretch out the front part of the body and remain motionless. In addition to their

The large maple spanworm is one of many inchworms that stretch out into the air and become "twigs," a very effective protection.

greenish or brownish colors, inchworms often have markings or projections of their bodies which resemble leaf scars or buds, further enhancing their twiglike appearance.

Other caterpillars, especially in the tropics, are disguised by their resemblance to bird droppings. The caterpillar of an African swallowtail has a rather shapeless outline. The front part of its body is blackish brown while the rounded rear end is white. As it rests in its perpetually bent position on the top of a leaf, it looks quite unlike a tasty caterpillar. Tropical moth caterpillars, too, may bear a remarkable resemblance to a bird dropping, while the young caterpillars of an African moth gather together on the leaf surface and collectively resemble a bird dropping.

Protective Devices

Instead of hiding, some caterpillars can defend themselves actively. Many have sharp spines which make them unpleasant fare. Some caterpillars with poisonous spines will arch backwards and actively attempt to drive their spines into an attacking enemy. Others have bright warning colors in addition to their spines. The caterpillar of one moth from Borneo is pink with bright blue and yellow markings. Its body bears tufts of black and yellow spines which cause terrible pain if touched. Any enemy which once encounters this unpleasant creature will remember to leave alone the next pink, spiny caterpillar it sees. Although the spines on many caterpillars are not poisonous, it is best to avoid contact with any hairy-looking caterpillar. The hairs on some can irritate human skin.

Red, black, and yellow are common warning colors in the animal kingdom. Bees, wasps, and hornets are usually black and yellow. Presumably, if a predator has a bad experience with a black and yellow insect, it will avoid others in the future. The poisonous caterpillar of the cinnabar moth is conspicuously banded with black and yellow, too.

It may seem hard to believe, but some caterpillars appear to defend themselves by scaring their enemies. Hawkmoth larvae, which are very large, often have conspicuous eyelike markings near their heads. These markings give the caterpillars a snakelike look and may well fool possible enemies. The snakelike appearance is enhanced in some species by their behavior when threatened. One kind, for example, swells up the front of its body, lets go with its front legs, and swings and lashes its body from side to side in snakelike fashion when disturbed. Some hawkmoth caterpillars have glands along the sides of their bodies which release an unpleasant bright green or yellow liquid if they are bothered.

Some swallowtail caterpillars have more refined repellent glands. If one of these insects is threatened, it rears up suddenly, lifting its front end. In case this doesn't startle its enemy, the caterpillar pushes out a brightly colored forked organ suggesting horns on the back of its neck. This organ is called the osmeterium and is covered with a strong-smelling chemical. If attacked by ants, the caterpillar swings around and wipes its osmeterium against them. They immediately run away, stopping as they flee to wipe the unpleasant stuff off their bodies.

8 · Unusual Lives

Here and there we have had hints of some rather exotic and unusual lepidopterans—a blood-sucking moth, a caterpillar which inhabits beehives and eats beeswax, and others. Unfortunately, many interesting lepidopterans have not been thoroughly studied by scientists, so it is not possible to fill in the details of their uncommon lives. Enough is known, however, about a few atypical kinds with interesting adaptations to say more about them.

It may be a surprise to learn that quite a few moths have aquatic larvae. Some live completely underwater and emerge into the air only as adult moths. Others are less adapted to an aquatic life, feeding on water plants and frequently coming up for air. The female of the most extremely aquatic moth never leaves the water at all, even as an adult. She has very small wings and swims using her legs. The male can fly and must return to the water to mate. Some aquatic caterpillars make houses for themselves from bits of dead leaves, while others construct floating rafts. They may lack gills entirely or have well-developed ones, with either blood vessels or air-filled tracheae branching out into the gills to gather oxygen.

One partly aquatic caterpillar is a pest of yellow water lilies along the east coast of the United States. The female moths lay their eggs on lily pads. The young caterpillars are leaf miners, feeding in the soft inside of the water lily leaf. As it feeds, the caterpillar eats its way toward the center of the leaf, entering the rib as a third instar caterpillar. By this time it is too large to remain inside the leaf as a miner. The caterpillar works its way toward the petiole as it feeds on the juicy midrib.

While living in the leaf, the caterpillar gets oxygen easily from holes in the top of the floating lily pad. But when it bores into the petiole it becomes submerged. Now it must back up every few minutes until the large last pair of spiracles are just above the surface. After filling its tracheae with fresh air, the caterpillar crawls back down and eats some more. It spends an average of only about three minutes feeding between trips to the surface and cannot stay under more than 15 minutes without air.

Once the caterpillar has completely consumed the soft parts of the petiole it must find a new one. It swims along the surface with surprising speed and little effort until it finds a fresh lily pad. This is a dangerous time for the caterpillar, for fish are quick to snap them up.

Despite the appetite of fish, the aquatic life seems to agree with these moths, for they can occur in such numbers in a lily pond that most of the lily pads are damaged or destroyed.

Staying Under Water

Along the west coast of this country live over a dozen species of related moths which are much more extremely aquatic. One common kind in northern California has two or three generations each year. The adults rest in the shade near the water during the day. Within a couple of hours after sunset, mating takes place. A night or two later, the female moth walks into the water to lay her eggs. Her whole body has an unreal, silvery look underwater, for it is completely covered with a thin layer of air. She can survive as long as twelve hours completely submerged and lays up to 300 eggs, attaching them in clusters to stones. After finishing her job, the female moth usually dies while still underwater.

The smooth eggs hatch out into larvae without gills, but later stages have well developed gills along their sides. By the second instar, the larvae build silken tents for themselves over cracks or holes in the rocks. There they feed on microscopic plants, protected by their tents from enemies. When they pupate, the larvae spin peculiar double cocoons. The inner cocoon fits tightly around the pupa. The outer one has holes in it which allow oxygen-bearing water to circulate around the inner cocoon. The adult moths emerge from their cocoons after midnight, swimming or floating up to the water's surface. They rest on floating debris while their wings expand and harden. Then they fly off to live their brief adult lives in the air.

Powerful Fliers

The sphinx moths (also called hawkmoths) have succeeded in a a very unmothlike life style. These strong-flying moths look like streamlined aircraft at rest, their long slim forewings resting at a swept-wing angle to their large but graceful bodies. Some have only a one-inch wingspan, but large ones may be 13½ centimeters (about 5½ inches) across, overlapping the size range of small hummingbirds. This should perhaps not be surprising, since sphinx moths live a life somewhat like that of hummingbirds. Their wings beat 25 to 30 times a second as they hover in front of flowers, sipping sweet nectar with their especially long probosces.

One of the best known sphinx moths is the tobacco sphinx, parent of the tobacco hornworm. Because of its unfortunate choice of a larval food plant, this moth has been the subject of some scientific study.

Sphinx moths fly from dusk into darkness. Because they lack ways to keep their body temperature at a constant level, warmer than the outside air, flying during the cooler night would seem a risky habit for

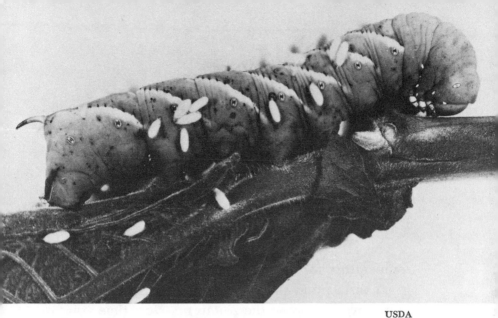

Hawkmoths, also called sphinx moths, are powerful fliers; their caterpillar is a stout-bodied creature. But like this tobacco hornworm, young of a hawkmoth species, it can become a victim of a wasp that lays eggs in its body, resulting in these attached wasp pupa cases and its subsequent death.

moths. But even though sphinx moth muscles must be 35-38° Celsius (95-100° F.) before the insects can fly, they are on the wing at air temperatures as low as 10° C. (50° F.). How is this possible?

When the sphinx moth is ready to fly, it mobilizes stored fat to generate heat. It raises its body and vibrates its wings together rapidly. The muscle contractions causing the vibration produce heat more quickly than the body loses it, as long as the air temperature is over 10° C. Warming up the body may take quite a while—as long as 15 minutes if the air temperature is 15° C. (59° F.). At higher air temperatures, it may take only a minute.

The sphinx moth has several adaptations which aid in its vital warmup. It is necessary for the moth to warm only its wing-bearing thorax for flight. The thorax is covered with a dense layer of long, hairlike scales which help insulate it. An air space between the thorax and the abdomen also helps keep heat from leaving the muscle-filled thorax.

This ability of sphinx moths to raise their own body temperature for flight is probably one reason for their great variety and success. Sphinx moths are found the world over except in the Antarctic. Next time you are outside around dusk, watch for these fascinating insects near flowers like columbine and honeysuckle. Maybe you'll be lucky enough to have one dart past you and hover, suspended on its vibrating wings, in front of a nectar-filled blossom.

Long-Lived Butterflies

The heliconiids (Heliconiidae), also called the passionflower butterflies, belong to a very unusual family. These tropical American forest fliers have evolved for so long in association with particular plants that their lives differ in several ways from the typical butterfly pattern. We've seen that the "typical" lepidopterans feed gluttonously as caterpillars and live no more than three or four weeks as nectar-feeding adults. Females may lay dozens of eggs a day during their short adult lives. But some passionflower butterflies, especially the closely related ones placed by scientists in the genus Heliconius, may live as long as six months. Females lay just a few eggs each day, but continue laying until they die.

There are two things about these butterflies that make a long and healthy life possible. In the first place, they are among the most distasteful of lepidopterans. The caterpillars feed on poisonous passionflower vines and apparently pass on the bad-tasting chemicals to the adult butterflies. These insects are usually warningly colored in black accented by yellow, orange, red, or white. They fly slowly through the forests flaunting their warning wings and often gather in large numbers at regular roosting places for the night. They are involved in some of the most interesting and complicated cases of mimicry ever studied (see the author's *Animal and Plant Mimicry* and Turner's article "A Tale of Two Butterflies," listed under Suggested Reading).

The second reason that passionflower butterflies can survive so long is their diet. In addition to nectar, they also gather pollen and are able to extract the vital protein-building amino acids from it. The butterfly collects a mass of pollen on its proboscis. Then it releases a drop of liquid, probably nectar, onto the pollen. The liquid causes the pollen to release amino acids which the butterfly then sucks back in with the liquid. The process takes time, and the butterfly works the pollen over for hours, coiling and uncoiling its proboscis.

Heliconius butterflies collect most of their pollen

from forest vines which are cucumber relatives. These vines produce a great deal of pollen throughout the year. Each butterfly has a regular pollen-collecting route which it covers, returning always to the same plants to see if there are flowers blooming each day. The female butterflies, which need more pollen to produce yolk for their eggs, go pollen-hunting mainly in the morning, while males are more likely to go out in the afternoon and collect a smaller quantity. The vines seem to rely on the regular collection routes of the butterflies for pollination of their flowers, and the butterflies depend on the year-around supply of pollen from the vines. Most female butterflies gain the greater part of the energy and materials to produce eggs while they are caterpillars. Most of the eggs which they lay are present in their ovaries when they emerge from their pupae. Yolk is added to them as they ripen by utilizing nutrients stored from caterpillar feeding. But the long-lived passionflower butterflies keep producing new eggs throughout their lives, using the vital amino acids they get from pollen.

The advantages to these butterflies in laying a few eggs each day over a period of months, instead of laying many eggs every day for days, are many. In the tropics there tend to be many different species of plants but only a few individuals of any one kind in an area. We are used to seeing vast meadows glowing with one or two kinds of wildflowers and huge forests dominated by one or two tree species. In the tropics it is different. There are many kinds of trees, with individuals of one kind very scattered and separate from one another. Smaller plants, too, have a sparser distribution than we are used to. A female Heliconius may have to fly a long distance to find an acceptable food plant for her larvae.

The butterflies must also get around the various ways passionflower vines have evolved of protecting themselves from the butterflies. The older leaves are tough, and young shoots make better caterpillar food. There is another reason for preferring young shoots, too. Passionflower vines (and many other tropical plants) make nectar available away from their flowers, which attracts ants and parasitic wasps to them. The ants walk all over the plants, attacking any eggs or caterpillars they find. The wasps lay their eggs on caterpillars. If the butterfly eggs and caterpillars are isolated far out on young shoots, they have less chance of being found by the ants and wasps.

On any one day, a single vine will not have very many tender young shoots for the female butterfly to lay eggs on. And because the passionflower vines are relatively scarce, she would have a hard time finding appropriate spots for very many eggs in one day. It is important, too, that not more than one egg be laid on one shoot, for Heliconius caterpillars are often cannibals, gobbling down any nearby rival caterpillars.

The female butterfly examines a shoot carefully before laying on it, possibly inspecting for caterpillars and previously laid eggs. Some passionflower vines appear to capitalize on this reluctance of female butterflies to lay eggs if other eggs are present. They have growths which bear a remarkable resemblance to butterfly eggs located on or near the new growing tips of the plants. While these "egg mimics" look to human eyes very much like Heliconius eggs, whether or not they actually fool the butterflies is not yet certain.

Long-Distance Fliers

Despite their fine flying ability, most lepidopterans spend their entire lives very near the place they hatched out. There are exceptions to this tendency, however, including the amazing monarch, which flies as far as 3200 kilometers (almost 2000 miles) or more to its overwintering grounds. But the monarch is not the only migrating lepidopteran. Butterflies such as the common cabbage butterfly, the painted lady, red admiral, and clouded yellow may migrate over a distance of a few hundred kilometers. Several common British butterflies migrate from North Africa and the Mediterranean, and every few years clouds of painted ladies are seen in various parts of the United States, all heading northward.

Several kinds of armyworm moths, which are serious crop pests of grains such as wheat and rice, are known to migrate, too. An individual Oriental armyworm moth can cover almost 1400 kilometers (about 869 miles). The total migration pattern for these moths is very complicated. The first generation of moths starts out in southern China in January and February, feeding on spring wheat. The adults then fly north in March and April. They lay their eggs on wheat, too. The second-generation moths also go north, but their offspring reverse the pattern and fly south in July and August. The fourth generation completes the cycle, traveling southward to lay their eggs on rice plants, where the larvae overwinter. The total distance covered, round trip, by the four generations of moths can be as far as 4600 kilometers (about 2858 miles).

The Champion Migrator

The most spectacular migrator of all lepidopterans, however, is the monarch butterfly. Not only does the monarch hold the distance record, its migrations are spectacular to see, with huge dense clouds of countless butterflies surging southward along the coasts for days at a time during the fall.

Several generations of monarchs are produced during the spring and summer months. These butterflies emerge from their chrysalises, mate, and die much like other butterflies. But as summer fades and the days grow shorter, the monarchs change. The combination of colder temperatures and shorter days causes the monarchs' bodies to produce juvenile hormone. In the adult butterfly, the juvenile hormone

The most efficient way of labeling monarchs to trace their flights is the wing label developed by Dr. F. A. Urquhart of Toronto; the tag will not come off or wash out in rain. Thousands of such taggings, suggested by bird-banding, have yielded valuable information about the monarch migrations.

stops the maturing of the ovaries and testes which would normally occur in the butterflies. Instead of spending their time courting and laying eggs, these last-generation butterflies gather to collect nectar and to sleep at night. Gradually the tendency to fly southward develops and by the middle of September the migration is in full swing.

For many years scientists have been marking monarchs along both coasts with numbered tags. If the tagged butterflies are captured later on farther south, the minimum distance flown by that butterfly can be determined. By using these tag experiments, the complete migration routes along the west coast were worked out long ago. This was fairly easy to do, for the human population all along the western coastal area is quite dense, and the overwintering sites are often in populated areas. The most famous one is in Pacific Grove, California, where the monarchs hang by the thousands from Monterey pines.

The migration routes in the eastern United States were also worked out. The butterflies flew progressively southward, with a few spending the winter in Florida. But the main migration route clearly led into remote parts of Mexico, where the trail was lost. No one knew where the vast majority of American monarchs spent the winter, despite years of tagging thousands of the insects. Now and then a tagged butterfly would turn up in Mexico, but the exact location or locations of the overwintering butterfly masses were unknown.

Then, in 1974, a butterfly specialist named Kenneth Brugger discovered an enormous colony of overwintering monarchs in the mountains of central Mexico. Dr. Brugger and his coworkers were very reluctant to reveal the exact location of this winter home, for they feared that publicity might draw people to the area, endangering the safety of the butterflies. But other scientists were anxious to study them, too, and some set off on their own hunt, knowing only the general area of the colony. In 1976, William Calvert, member of another research team, found what is probably the same butterfly colony, and the group was able to study it in some detail. They dubbed the location "Site Alpha."

The scene at Site Alpha was amazing—almost four acres of trees absolutely covered with butterflies. The cyprus trees were almost unrecognizable, for their needles were so laden with butterflies that they couldn't be seen. Some trees were bent over from the weight of the insects. Tree trunks were so covered with monarchs, all resting in the same position, that the bark was completely obscured. Any estimate of the number of butterflies at Site Alpha is a wild guess, for even to figure out how many individuals are draped on one tree would be a challenge. But by using figures from studies of overwintering butterflies in California, the scientists estimate that at least 13.8 million butterflies spend the winter at Site Alpha, and that there may be as many as 100 million insects there.

The climate at Site Alpha is perfect for the overwintering monarchs. It is a forested area, located at an elevation of over 2300 meters (about 7545 feet). Because of its cloud-high location, it has very high humidity, which protects the insects from drying out as they land on the trees. The temperature variation is slight, with minimum night temperatures above freezing and maximum daytime temperatures usually just below the level at which the butterflies could fly. Therefore the insects spend the winter in what amounts to a natural refrigerator, keeping them inactive so that

At a Mexican overwintering site, Dr. Lincoln Brower examines some of the thousands of monarchs clinging to tree trunks.
GEORGE LEPP

they conserve as much energy as possible for their northward flight in the spring. On sunny days some of the butterflies are able to fly to nearby springs and drink water from the damp creek edges. They keep their wings spread, basking in the sunlight, so that their bodies are warm enough to fly back to the trees.

Little is known about the return flight of the monarchs in the spring. It does not occur in large groups like the fall migration, so it is harder to keep track of. The insects appear to fly northward individually, with females laying their eggs as they go. Because of the battered and worn condition of some monarchs when they reach the northern part of their range, some scientists believe that the same butterflies which flew 3200 kilometers (nearly 2000 miles) or more in the fall may make the entire return trip in the spring. Others think that this is just too far for even a monarch to travel. They believe that butterflies which emerge in the early spring in the South fly north a certain distance and reproduce, until butterflies a generation or more removed from the fall migrators reach the northern limits of the monarch's range.

Since the overwintering grounds have only recently been discovered, mark and recapture studies of the return trip have yet to be carried out. Now that at least one overwintering site is known, investigators hope that marking of the butterflies can be done so that more will be learned about the return flights of this remarkable insect.

9 · Enemies and Friends

Birds and other vertebrate hunters aren't the only enemies of lepidopterans. A great number of insects attack them, too. Ants may devour over 90 per cent of the eggs of some butterflies before they even hatch. Paper wasps paralyze caterpillars and carry them to their nests where they chew them up and feed them to their larvae. Crab spiders and mantises, camouflaged within flowers, grab landing butterflies and consume them. But perhaps the most troublesome insect enemies of lepidopterans are insect parasites, especially various kinds of wasps and flies. Some of these have especially interesting adaptations to their way of life.

You may be familiar with insects popularly called "ichneumon flies." These are not flies at all but rather, parasitic wasps which attack various insects. We think of wasps as large black and yellow creatures which live in paper nest colonies. But most wasps are actually solitary insects which do not make paper nests at all.

Social wasps can deliver quite a painful sting, but the solitary wasps cannot hurt humans. The wasp "stinger" is really an egg-laying tool called the ovipositor. Paper wasp and honeybee workers have their ovipositors modified into especially effective stingers, strong enough to attack vertebrates which may threaten their nests. Solitary wasps have no nest to protect, and use their ovipositors to lay their eggs and to sting their prey.

Ichneumon wasps often have very long ovipositors which enable them to attack caterpillars or other prey deep inside host plants. This organ in some kinds is even longer than the body. Icneumon wasps and their close relatives, the braconids, often parasitize familiar caterpillars such as the cabbage worm and tomato hornworm. The females wasp lays several eggs

A *braconid wasp,* Apanteles rubecula, *laying eggs in the larva of a cabbage butterfly.*   USDA

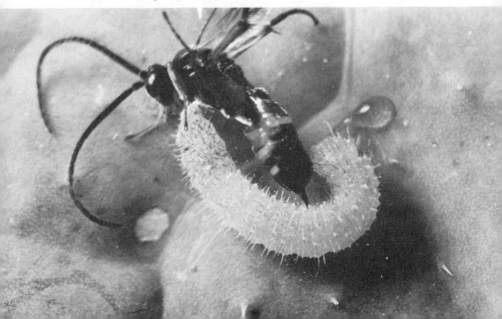

inside the blood-filled body cavity of the caterpillar. The wasp larvae feed on the caterpillar from within, first attacking the fat body where nutrients are stored and later consuming the vital organs, killing the caterpillar before it can pupate. The mature wasp larvae burrow out through the caterpillar and pupate inside small cocoons attached to its dead and shriveled body.

Deadly Midgets

Many parasites of lepidopterans belong to a group of wasps called chalcids. These are very small insects, usually only two to three millimeters (about ⅒ inch) long. They look like tiny metallic green or black flies. Some chalcids are very particular about their hosts, while others are able to attack a wide variety of insects. For example, one kind infests only a few closely related moths which feed on rushes, while another will attack a great variety of leaf-mining insects, including caterpillars.

Some chalcids paralyze their prey and then lay their eggs on the outside of the body. The helpless host insect lives on for quite a while, being eaten alive by the wasp larvae. Other chalcids lay their eggs inside the caterpillar, injecting them with their long ovipositors.

Chalcids which attack leaf-miners lay just one egg inside the caterpillar. While the wasp larva is developing, it does not deposit any wastes which might con-

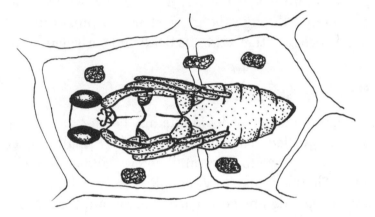

Pupa of a chalcid wasp inside a leaf. The wasp larva has eaten a leaf-mining caterpillar and pupated within a circle of pillars formed from its waste pellets. Above is a side view of the wasp pupa, showing how the pillars support the leaf and protect the pupa. Below is a view from underneath, showing details of the protected insect. Eyes, mouth, and legs can be clearly seen. Drawing by the author.

taminate its food. And before it pupates, it eats every last bit of the caterpillar. That way, no dead tissue is nearby to rot and contaminate the wasp pupa. All the wastes from the wasp larva's development are released just before it pupates. The larva of some chalcids makes a circle of minute pillars with the waste pellets. It pupates inside the circle. When the pellets dry and harden, they protect the wasp pupa from the collapse of the leaf as it dries.

Thousands of chalcids may develop inside a large caterpillar when the female wasp has laid only a few eggs in it. Each egg develops into a chain of as many as 500 cell clumps. The chains fragment in the blood space of the caterpillar, and each clump then develops into an individual chalcid larva. By the time the chalcids are ready to pupate, the poor victim is nothing but a swollen bag teeming with chalcid larvae.

Lepidopteran Diseases

Caterpillars, like people, are susceptible to diseases caused by viruses and bacteria. One bacterial disease, caused by a microbe named *Bacillus thurengensis,* is especially deadly and very contagious. Caterpillars of several lepidopterans, including the cabbage butterfly and other pests, can catch it. Scientists have capitalized on this weakness and have developed a concoction consisting of millions of bacteria which farmers and gardeners can spray on their crops. The bacteria affect the caterpillars almost immediately, inhibiting their feeding and finally killing them. Apparently the caterpillars are affected by toxic crystals in the bacterial spray rather than by infection with the bacteria themselves. This spray is a much better means of pest control than poisonous chemicals, for it affects only the pest caterpillars and not helpful insects such as bees and parasitic wasps. The one drawback of it is, however, that it must be sprayed several times each growing season.

Virus sprays are also being developed as tools for pest caterpillar control. The viruses are more specific about which insects they affect than is *Bacillus thurengensis*. They do not kill as quickly as the bacteria, but they are more persistent. Once an area has been sprayed, the viruses may stay around to infect caterpillars for years. As more and more such diseases are harnessed to attack unwanted insect pests, use of dangerous general insecticides will lessen so that beneficial insects are not harmed.

Living with Ants

While ants are enemies of many lepidopterans, some moths and butterflies have evolved ways of living in harmony with the enemy. Ants are generally quite aggressive creatures, attacking other insects and spiders which enter their domain. Many kinds are big enough to give bites painful even to vertebrate predators and can spray unpleasant acid when disturbed. For these reasons, most other creatures leave ants alone. Those lepidopterans which have found ways to associate with them without inviting attack gain protection from the bad reputation of their hosts.

Species in nine different lepidopteran families live with ants in one way or another. Some have caterpillars which produce honeydew which the ants can drink, much as aphids do. Others live within the ant nest as larvae, feeding on the ant brood. When it emerges from its pupa, the adult butterfly or moth must get out of the nest without being attacked by the ants. Several kinds have evolved heavily scaled bodies with long, hairy scales on their antennae, mouthparts, and legs as well as their wings. If ants attack, they get a mouthful of scales and quickly retreat to clean up while the lepidopteran escapes.

Two butterfly families, the Lycaenidae and Riodinidae, have a vast variety of relationships with ants that range from mere sharing of the same tree trunk to providing food for one another. Surprisingly enough, Lycaenidae is the largest of all butterfly families, with around 6000 different species. Because of their small size, these interesting creatures often go unnoticed as they flutter past our feet. But there are many common North American species. Once you begin to notice them, you will see how numerous they really are. The lycaenids are divided into three groups, the blues, the hairstreaks, and the coppers. These names describe quite well the appearance of the butterflies—blues have lovely bright blue or purple wings; coppers generally have glowing coppery-orange wings; hairstreaks have delicate "tails" on their hindwings which are thought to be antenna mimics, used to confuse predators.

The great majority of these butterflies have some

sort of relationship with ants. Species of one group from Africa lay their eggs on trees which harbor ant nests. The caterpillars feed on lichens growing on the trunk. They stay among the ant columns which stream up and down the trunk. Moth caterpillars also live on the same tree trunks, and the butterfly caterpillars appear to mimic them. Unlike their relatives, these butterfly caterpillars have spines and red, green, and yellow bodies. The moth larva spines can sting, but the butterfly ones cannot. Perhaps the spines protect the moth larvae from ant attack, and the similarity of the butterfly caterpillars protects them, too. In any case, the ants completely ignore the caterpillars. But by living among the columns of aggressive ants, the caterpillars are probably protected from their enemies.

Caterpillar "Cows"

Ants are famous for the way they care for aphids and scale insects, protecting them like herds of cattle and "milking" them for sweet honeydew. Many lycaenid caterpillars are tended by ants just like aphids. They have glands on their backs which produce a sweet liquid that the ants lick away. In exchange for this, the caterpillars gain protection from enemies. Some kinds are so dependent on ants that they die if the sweet secretion is not removed. If raised in captivity, these caterpillars must frequently be gently brushed to remove the secretion or it will crust and develop molds which kill the caterpillar.

Some of these larvae are especially well tended by the ants, which build protective "sheds" over them. The ants drive the caterpillars out of the shelters in the evening to feed on plants and back in again during the day to rest. Some species share their shelters with other ant "cattle" such as mealybugs.

Unfortunately, little is known about the relationships of most such butterflies with their ant hosts. But a few life histories are known in more detail. One Mexican metalmark (Riodinidae) with an especially intimate association with its ant hosts was carefully studied by Dr. Gary Ross. The butterflies lay their eggs on small bushes which have nectar glands that

The larva of one species of metalmark butterfly, Anatole rossi, *is cared for by ants that lick honeydew from it, as certain ants do with aphids and scale insects.* DR. GARY N. ROSS

attract ants. For the first two instars the caterpillar lives alone, feeding at night on the leaves and resting during the daytime on a silken mat it spins on the underside of a leaf.

When the caterpillar molts into the third instar, a remarkable transformation occurs. Now it has three different sorts of structures which are involved in its relationship to ants. It has a pair of honey glands on its abdomen which produce sweet liquid for the ants to drink. It has a pair of strange bumps which can be pushed out along its sides. These appear to produce a substance which attracts the ants. But they also are covered with sharp spines which may keep the ants away from the vulnerable head of the caterpillar. The third set of ant-related organs is a pair of antennalike projections which extend over the head and are vibrated by the caterpillar. Just what effect they may have on the ants is not known.

Very shortly after molting, the third-instar larva is found and "adopted" by ants of a species common in the area. These ants have a defensive acid secretion and are quite aggressive. They appear to rely completely on the sweet fluid from caterpillars and aphid honeydew for their nourishment. When a worker ant discovers a caterpillar, it runs excitedly all over its find, pausing now and then to drink from the fluid glands. Soon it wanders off onto the ground until it finds a fellow worker ant. They return to the caterpillar and both run over it, again drinking. After a while they

*The ants dig a pit for the metalmark caterpillar and keep it
a prisoner there during the day, releasing it each evening.*

descend to the base of the plant and dig a shallow de-
pression in the ground. This project takes several
hours, during which they periodically return to check
their new captive and drink more fluid from it.

Once their excavation is finished, they return to the
caterpillar and run over and about it until it crawls

down the plant stem. They follow it into the pen they have built and seal it off. During this whole operation, more ants may join in so that as many as six ants end up sealed in the pen with the caterpillar. From then on the routine is set. Every evening the ants open up the pen and crawl out over the plant, grabbing any insects or spiders they find and dumping them well away from the area. They spend 10 to 15 minutes policing the plant and when it is completely cleared of other creatures, the caterpillar emerges from its pen and crawls out to feed.

While the caterpillar eats, the ants stay with it, running over its body and the adjacent leaves and drinking its fluid. As dawn approaches, the ants become excited and run about more and more until the caterpillar follows their lead and restlessly crawls about until it heads down the stem and back to its pen. Before the sun rises, the caterpillar and its guardians are again sealed within their protected cave for the day.

Dr. Ross showed the strong attachment of the ants to the caterpillar by doing some simple experiments. If he removed the caterpillar, the ants abandoned the pen within 90 minutes and wandered away. If the larva was moved to a nearby plant, the ants would rediscover it and build a new pen within six hours, even if he had moved the caterpillar to a plant a full three feet (almost a meter) away. The caterpillar, however, can do fine without the ants as long as it is protected from enemies. A caterpillar on a plant surrounded by a net cage reverts to its earlier behavior pattern, spinning a silk mat on the underside of a leaf and staying there rather than crawling down the stem to the pen below. If the caterpillar is removed to a plant away from an ant colony, however, it does not last long. Other kinds of ants with big appetites for caterpillars attack it quickly, stinging it and dragging it off to their nest.

As the weather gets colder in the fall, the ants enlarge the pen, making it wider and deeper until by February it is a crooked tunnel up to 15 centimeters (six inches) deep. By this time the plant is little more than a skeleton, with only a few leaves left. Now the caterpillar leaves its protected pen only occasionally, emerging every few days for a brief period to nibble on the remains of the plant. The leaves are all gone by spring, and it has only stems left to munch on.

When the caterpillar is young, the ants caring for it leave infrequently. Every few days one wanders off and does not return, being replaced by another from the mother colony. During the winter and spring, while the caterpillar is sluggish and hardly feeding, the attendant ants change every two hours or so. The caterpillar is probably producing little sweet fluid at this time. Soon it pupates, hanging head down, attached to a root within the pen. After the pupa is formed, the ants remove the old caterpillar skin from the pen and watch over the pupa. It has a pair of glands which appear to secrete an attractive chemical and a pair of sound-producing organs which also attract the ants. But it does not give any more food, so the attendant ants trade places frequently. About two days before the butterfly emerges, the ants abandon the pupa. When the butterfly comes out, it climbs alone out of the protective pen into the springtime sunlight.

A Guest in the Nest

The large blue butterfly (this is its straightforward common name) of Britain has a fascinating life cycle. It can survive only in areas where both wild thyme and one of two species of red ant are both found together. The female butterfly lays her eggs individually on thyme flowers. The larvae feed on the flowers during the first three instars and will attack and eat other caterpillars as well if they come across them. After molting into the fourth instar, a drastic change in behavior of the caterpillar occurs. It leaves the thyme plants and wanders about over the ground. Only if it is found by an ant can it survive to become a butterfly. If an ant does encounter the caterpillar, it strokes it with its antennae. This causes the caterpillar to release generous quantities of liquid from a gland on its back, which the ant drinks. The ant walks around and returns to stroke and feed. This may go on for an hour or more until suddenly the caterpillar swells up its front end into a fat hump, while the rear end remains unchanged. This acts as a signal to the ant to grab the caterpillar in its jaws and carry it away to the ant nest.

Once inside the nest, the caterpillar feeds on ant larvae. In only four or five weeks it triples its size and becomes a very pale, fat, grublike creature. Despite its great growth, it does not molt. As winter approaches, the caterpillar retires to a secluded place deep within the nest and hibernates. In the spring it resumes feeding and continues to eat and grow until May or early June. The caterpillar was a very small creature, only 3.2 millimeters (less than ⅒ inch) long when it entered the nest. Now it is 15 millimeters (over a half inch) long and pupates within the galleries of the nest. When the butterfly leaves, it climbs up through the passageways to the outside before opening its wings.

10 · Pleasing and Harming Humans

Human attitudes toward butterflies are very different from those toward moths. We think of butterflies as beautiful symbols of easygoing freedom. Butterflies have adorned our works of art since they were first painted on Egyptian tombs in 3000 B.C. Artists around the world have been charmed by the grace and elegance of these insects' wings. Butterfly images occur in the pottery of England, the silk embroidery of China, the batik of Java. In many societies, butterflies were thought to be the souls of the dead, and North American Indians ensured the sweet dreams of their babies by embroidering butterflies on their caps.

Perhaps the greatest impact of butterflies on humans, however, has been through butterfly-collecting. This popular hobby inspired many jungle journeys in search of such majestic beauties as the morphos and birdwings. Much of our knowledge of tropical butterflies today comes not from scientists but from dedicated amateur collectors and, more recently, photographers. Unfortunately, the collector's passion may lead to overcollecting of rare species. When a dealer can get more than $1000 for one giant birdwing specimen, the incentive to capture even rare species protected by law is great.

Most scientists feel, however, that the greatest danger to butterfly species does not come from enthusiastic collecting. These lepidopterans are often the innocent victims of heavy pesticide use. They appear to be much less abundant in gardens and fields than they used to be. The destruction of their habitats also results in their drastic decline. As jungles are leveled and meadows plowed, the plants upon which butterflies rely disappear and with them go the winged beauties.

Butterfly-collecting, responsibly carried out, can be a very rewarding and informative hobby. If you are interested in the details of collecting and preserving specimens, see the list of books under Suggested Reading. Nowadays more and more people are collecting butterflies with a camera rather than with a net. Not only is there the satisfaction of leaving your specimen alive and well, there is the greater challenge of capturing the living, flying insect on film.

Helpful and Harmful Moths

Even though moths are far more numerous than butterflies, few people give them much thought. Those "in the know," however, find moths every bit as fascinating (and sometimes beautiful) as butterflies (for an exciting example, see Sandved's "Magnificent Deceivers: Moths" under Suggested Reading). Our relationships with moths have certainly been more intimate over the ages. For close to 4000 years, silkworm moths have been making material for our clothes while clothes moths have been eating them. Various moths have been destroying crops ever since people began farming.

The silkworm moth is the only truly domesticated insect. Honeybees are kept in manufactured hives for their honey, but they can survive perfectly well in the wild. And anyone who has disturbed a hive of domesticated bees knows their sting is just as painful and freely given as that of wild bees. But the silkworm has lived under human cultivation for so long that it is completely dependent on humans for survival. Silkworm culture began around 1800 B.C. when the wife of a Chinese emperor studied the moths and devised a means of raising them in captivity and unwinding the silk from their cocoons. For hundreds of years, silkworm culture was a well kept secret, and the Chinese were able to command high prices for their lovely, satiny fabric. Eventually the secret got out when some monks smuggled a few silkworms out of China and took them to Constantinople.

Over the centuries, silkworms have been carefully bred into different strains producing various kinds and

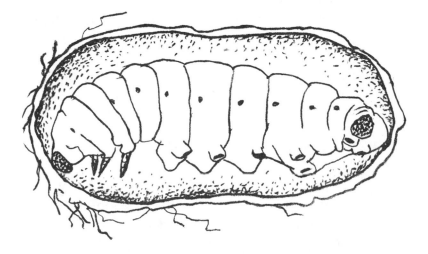

Bombyx mori, *the silk "worm" of China, is now entirely do-*
mesticated, and has been bred so long for producing the
highest quality of silk that it depends on humans to survive.
This shows a silky cocoon cut open to reveal the caterpillar
before it pupates.

colors of silk. The moths have lost their ability to fly,
and moths and caterpillars alike have acquired a white
color. Silkworms are raised in open trays and fed hand-
picked mulberry leaves. After they pupate and spin
their cocoons, the cocoons are removed and boiled.
The boiling kills the pupae and loosens the silk so
that it can be more easily unwound from the cocoon.
The silk in a single cocoon consists of one continuous
fiber as long as 300 meters (about 984 feet). In an-
cient China the boiled pupae were eaten so that no
part of the cocoon was wasted. Of course, a few

cocoons are left to develop into moths for breeding. The moths have been selected for the quality and quantity of the silk for so long that the moths cannot emerge from the large, tough cocoons without human help.

Holes in Clothes

While the silkworms are busily spinning silk, clothes moths are quietly chewing away at wool, silk, and felt garments. Despite their importance to humans, the habits of clothes moths are actually little known. There are three kinds—the webbing clothes moth, the casemaking clothes moth, and the carpet moth. The carpet moth is especially destructive, building long silken galleries through the fabric it infests. Fortunately, this pest is rare in the United States. The webbing clothes moth is the most familiar over much of this country. The adult moth has plain, straw-colored wings which it holds rolled over its body. The very small caterpillars eat little holes in clothing such as sweaters. The holes may be small, but they are difficult to repair in knitted fabrics without leaving unattractive "scars."

The casemaking clothes moth can be very destructive over a short period of time. The caterpillars of this little moth live inside a protective silken case, much like a cocoon. If they are living in a woolen carpet, the larvae may climb up the walls of a room to pupate.

The first sign a homeowner may see that his carpet has holes in it under the furniture is the strange, brownish cases of the pupae which appear mysteriously on his walls.

The Gypsy Moth

Often, our most serious pests are imported species, native to other parts of the world and introduced accidentally into our country. The Japanese beetle and the cabbage butterfly are two unpleasant examples. The gypsy moth, one of our most alarming enemies, is another. During the 1800s, many people were trying to find a silk moth which would survive in this country and produce marketable silk. These attempts to breed silkworms led to the accidental introduction into the wild of several moths, including the gypsy moth. (And none of them were useful as silk producers.) An entomologist in 1869 brought some gypsy moths into his home in Bedford, Massachusetts, hoping to breed them for silk production. Some escaped and although he notified the authorities, nothing was done for 12 years even though the moths were known to be pests of forest and shade trees in Europe.

It wasn't long before the moth took hold, at first along the street where he lived and then over greater and greater areas of the northeast. The caterpillars are amazingly efficient at leaf-eating. One resident in

1889 said that when he left his home in June the trees in his yard were healthy. But when he returned three days later their leaves were almost all gone.

The female gypsy moth cannot fly, but she produces a powerful sex attractant which brings in males from far away. After mating, she lays masses of from 100 to 600 eggs on trees, fences, or buildings. Neither the male nor the female feeds, and both die soon after mating. The caterpillars hatch out in spring, when the leaves are tender. They spread easily from tree to tree, for when young they spin a thread from which they hang. The thread with the attached caterpillar may be carried for miles by the wind. The caterpillars can feed on leaves of many different trees including apple, hawthorn, willow, and others. Oak seems to be a particular favorite. The moths have been able to spread from their point of importation to occupy over 200,000 square miles of forest and continue to spread.

Fortunately, more and more control measures are being developed. DDT used to be used in massive amounts in attempts to control the gypsy moth. *Bacillus thurengensis* kills the larvae, and various parasites have been introduced, including a wasp which parasitizes the eggs, a fly which attacks the caterpillars, and a predatory beetle. The sex attractant of the gypsy moth can be manufactured in the laboratory and is now used to attract males to see if the moths have invaded new territory. Researchers hope that soon the sex attractant can be used to control moth populations as well.

Crop Pests

Such enemies of crops and forest trees as bollworms, cankerworms, loopers, webworms, and leaf rollers, as well as many leaf miners and wood borers, are moth caterpillars. These pests cause millions of dollars' worth of damage every year to crops and trees. Despite the heavy use of such pesticides as DDT and dieldrin, these pests are still with us. There are several reasons for this. Two reasons in particular show why we must continue to develop other means of pest control besides general pesticides.

A rather exotic example will show both points. Other examples could be used, but this particular one involves several lepidopteran pests at once. In Ceylon, tea is an important crop. One major pest is a shoot-boring caterpillar which used to be controlled by careful culturing techniques until the 1950s, when dieldrin came into use. Then the real problems started. Dieldrin controlled the shoot borers well. But it killed off parasitic wasps which had previously been imported to control another pesky caterpillar, the tea tortrix. In order to control the tea tortrix, now that the wasps were gone, DDT was necessary. For several years, a combination of dieldrin, followed by DDT, worked pretty well, except that the DDT seemed to encourage mite attacks. Then the tea tortrix appeared to develop some tolerance to DDT, and it became harder to control. At the same time, large outbreaks of two other leaf-eating caterpillars started occurring. One had previously been only a minor pest and the second seemed to be completely new. These new pests combined were causing more damage than the original two pests, the shoot borer and the tea tortrix combined! All of these problems with the tea pests were shown by further research to be due to pesticide use.

The first major problem with pesticides is that they kill off all insects, not just the pests. The tea tortrix populations rose after tea was treated with dieldrin because its parasites were killed off. They were more susceptible to the poison than the tea tortrix was, so now the caterpillar was free to flourish without natural enemies. The later increase in caterpillars which had not been serious pests before was probably due to the same phenomenon. The enemies of the pests were more susceptible to the pesticides than were the pests.

The second problem with pesticides is that through continuing evolution insects can develop tolerance or outright immunity to them. This has become a serious problem in several parts of the world today, where mosquitos have become tolerant to DDT, and malaria is on the rise again. In the tea example, the resurgence of the tea tortrix after years of pesticide use was due to development of tolerance to the poison.

Biological Control

If pesticides are not the final answer, what is? Fortunately, scientists have been working very hard to develop other ways of controlling pests. We've already seen how the sex attractant of the pink bollworm moth is used to confuse the reproduction of this important pest. Sex attractants are being developed for similar control of pests such as the gypsy moth. Sex attractants are especially good for pest control because they are very specific and affect only one or a very few closely related species. They are completely harmless to all living things and are used in very small quantities. It would be just about impossible for a pest to develop resistance to its own sex attractant; how, then, could it find a mate?

We've also seen that bacteria and viruses specific to insects can be used for control. So far, only the bacterial spray has been licensed for use, but the more specific and persistent viruses will, one hopes, be available soon. While these organisms do kill their hosts and sometimes other insects, they are still very preferable to poisons, for they affect a much narrower range of living things and are harmless to vertebrate animals.

We've seen that natural enemies of pests can also be used for biological control. Parasitic wasps and flies are often effective in holding down the populations of

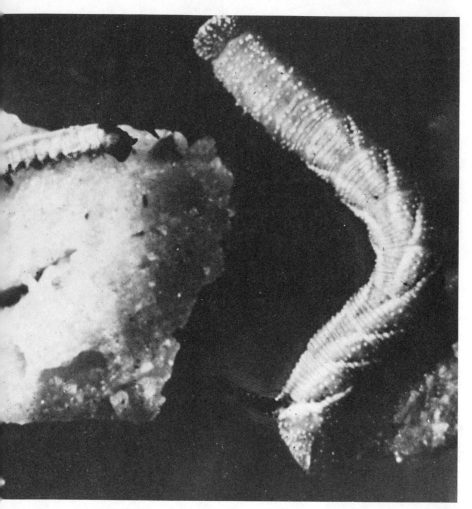

One method of biological control is to spray molting hormone on caterpillars' food plants, in excessive quantities and at the wrong time for normal development. Both the normal tobacco hornworm at right and the dwarfed one at left (at top edge of a food article) are the same age, but the small one was slowed in development and made unable to reproduce by getting molting hormone in its diet.

pests, as they did for the tea tortrix in Ceylon before the use of dieldrin. Natural enemies can be encouraged by the farmer, too, if he understands something of their life cycles. A recent study showed, for example, that apple orchards which were not sprayed with pesticides and had lots of wild flowers growing between the trees had many more enemies of codling moths and tent caterpillars present than did neat, well-manicured orchards. In the orchards with abundant wild flowers, four times as many pest eggs were parasitized as in ones with few flowers. Five times as many codling moth larvae and 18 times as many tent caterpillar pupae were parasitized. The adult parasitic wasps feed on flower nectar. They can thrive where plenty of wild flowers bloom. But if there are few flowers, they do not have enough food. They avoid such places and won't lay eggs there.

As we come to have a better understanding of how the different parts of nature—food plants, flowers, natural enemies, insect diseases, and insect pests interact, we can find healthier and more satisfactory ways of controlling moths and other insect pests. Then perhaps such usually harmless and attractive insects as butterflies will again become common in our gardens and wild places. We will have learned to appreciate all the world's creatures and respect the ways they interact with one another to keep nature in balance.

Glossary

abdomen: The back part of an insect's body, which contains most of the internal organs.

aeropyles: Microscopic holes in an insect egg which allow oxygen into the egg.

bagworm: The larva of a moth which builds a "house" for itself out of bits of leaves and silk; the female moths are flightless.

blue (a kind of butterfly): Member of a family Lycaenidae, the largest butterfly family. Most blues have some sort of relationship with ants.

brain hormone: A hormone from the head of an insect which stimulates the release of ecdysone (molting hormone).

chorion: The tough outer "shell" of an insect egg.

chrysalis: The pupa of a butterfly.

cuticle: The hard outer covering of an insect's body.

danaid: Butterfly in the family Danaidae; milkweed butterflies such as the monarch and the queen.

diapause: The "resting" period of an insect which allows it to survive the winter or the dry season.

ecdysone: The molting hormone of insects which causes them to shed their cuticles.

ganglion: A bundle of nerve cells.

hairpencils: Elaborate "brushes" possessed by males of some butterflies and moths which release chemicals affecting behavior of the female.

hawkmoth: A moth in the family Sphingidae which beats its wings very fast and can hover in front of flowers.

Heliconius: Genus (a related group) of tropical butterflies many of which are very long-lived and distasteful.

instar: A stage in caterpillar life between molts.

ithomiid: Butterfly in the tropical family Ithomiidae, with narrow wings and thin bodies. Many are almost transparent while others are brightly colored.

juvenile hormone: Chemical produced in an insect's body which inhibits development of adult structures.

leaf miner: An insect which tunnels between the upper and lower surfaces of a leaf, producing patterns which are typical for its kind; many moth caterpillars are leaf miners.

mandibles: Insect jaws, prominent in caterpillars but absent in adult butterflies and moths.

maxillae: Mouthparts used by the caterpillar to help hold its food. In the adult butterfly and moth, the maxillae are long and hollow, forming the sucking proboscis.

metalmark: Butterfly in the family Riodinidae, many of which have special relationships with ants.

milkweed butterfly: Member of the family Danaidae, which feed on milkweeds as caterpillars.

osmeterium: Defensive organ of some swallowtail caterpillars, consisting of a pair of "horns" which can be pushed out and which are coated with an unpleasant fluid.

petiole: The "stem" of a plant leaf.

proboscis: The long sucking organ of lepidopterans; it consists of two halves which are joined together, forming a hollow "straw" between them.

pupa: The third, outwardly inactive stage in the lepidopteran life cycle, during which the caterpillar is transformed into an adult insect.

sensilla: (sing., *sensillum*) The individual sense organs on the antennae or other part of the insect body.

skipper: Lepidopteran in the family Hesperiidae, considered by most to be a butterfly but described by others as somewhere between a moth and a butterfly.

sphinx moth: Another name for hawkmoth.

spiracle: An opening in the insect body allowing air into the tracheae.

thorax: The middle section of the insect body which bears the wings and legs.

tracheae: The air-filled tubes in an insect's body which bring oxygen to the cells and take carbon dioxide away.

Suggested Reading

Books

Jo Brewer (text) and Kjell B. Sandved (photographs), *Butterflies* (Abrams, N.Y., 1976). Good text and gorgeous photographs.

Philip S. Callahan, *Insects and How They Function* (Holiday House, N.Y., 1971). Information on flight, senses, digestion, etc., of all insects. Good illustrations, many made by the scanning electron microscope.

Thomas C. Emmel, *Butterflies: Their World, Their Life Cycle, Their Behavior* (Chanticleer/Knopf, N.Y., 1975). A few minor errors in the text, but beautiful photographs. Includes information on collecting and photographing butterflies.

Robert Godden, *All Color Book of Butterflies* (Bounty Books, N.Y., 1974). Inexpensive, geographically arranged book by an expert, with fine photos.

———, *The Wonderful World of Butterflies and Moths* (Hamlyn/America—A&W Publishers, N.Y., 1977). Interesting text, fine photos, and a section on raising lepidopterans in captivity.

W. J. Holland, *The Moth Book* (Dover, N.Y., 1968, rev. ed.; paperback). An updated edition of a book well known for over 60 years; some 1500 moths shown in full-color photographs.

David G. Measures, *Bright Wings of Summer: Watching Butterflies* (Prentice-Hall, Englewood Cliffs, N.J., 1976). Emphasizes the joys of observing rather than collecting, based on ten years of watching British butterflies.

Dorothy Hinshaw Patent, *Animal and Plant Mimicry* (Holiday House, N.Y., 1978). Contains many examples of mimicry among butterflies, moths, and other insects.

Kjell B. Sandved and Michael G. Emsley, *Butterfly Magic* (hardback: Viking Press, N.Y, 1975; paperback: Penguin Books, Baltimore, Md., 1976). Inexpensive in paperback, with especially striking photographs of butterfly scales in close-up.

Paul Smart, *The International Butterfly Book* (Crowell, N.Y., 1975). Good text, including information on collecting and breeding. Photos of over 2000 species, arranged by families.

Dorothy Sterling, *Caterpillars* (Doubleday, Garden City, N.Y., 1961)

Allan Watson and Paul E. S. Whalley, *The Dictionary of Butterflies and Moths in Color* (McGraw-Hill, N.Y., 1975)

Guide Books

Paul Ehrlich and Anne H. Ehrlich, *How to Know the Butterflies* (Wm. C. Brown, Dubuque, Iowa, 1961).

William H. Howe, ed., *The Butterflies of North America* (Doubleday, N.Y., 1976)

Alexander B. Klots, *A Field Guide to the Butterflies of North America East of the Great Plains* (Houghton Mifflin, Boston, 1977)

Arthur C. Smith, *Western Butterflies* (Lane Book Company, Menlo Park, Cal., 1961). Also has information on collecting. Identification is arranged by habitat.

Paul Villiard, *Moths and How to Rear Them* (Dover, N.Y., 1969; paperback). Contains 354 photographs; describes 88 species that the author personally raised for observation, experiment, and insect photography.

Magazine Articles

Martin Birch, "Persuasive Scents in Moth Sex Life," *Natural History,* Nov. 1970

T. A. Bishop and Laurence M. Cook, "Moths, Melanism, and Clean Air," *Scientific American,* Jan. 1975

Lincoln P. Brower, "Ecological Chemistry," *Scientific American,* Feb. 1969. About poisonous butterflies such as the monarch and their food plants.

———, "Monarch Migration," *Natural History,* June 1977

Treat Davidson, "Moths that Behave Like Hummingbirds," *National Geographic,* June 1965

Paul R. Ehrlich and Peter H. Raven, "Butterflies and Plants," *Scientific American,* June 1967

Bernard Heinrich and George A. Bartholomew, "Temperature Control in Flying Moths," *Scientific American,* June 1970

H. E. Hinton, "Insect Eggshells," *Scientific American,* August 1970

Alexander B. Klots, "On the Character of Color," *Natural History,* June 1963. Discusses the colors of lepidopteran wings and their functions.

Robert M. Pyle, "Silk Moth of the Railroad Yards," *Natural History,* May 1975. About the beautiful introduced Cynthia moth.

Kenneth D. Roeder, "Moths and Ultrasound," *Scientific American,* April 1965. How moths evade bats.

Kjell B. Sandved, "Magnificent Deceivers: Moths," *International Wildlife,* Nov. 1975. Beautiful photos of amazing moth camouflage.

Dietrich Schneider, "The Sex-Attractant Receptor of Moths," *Scientific American,* July 1974

John R. G. Turner, "A Tale of Two Butterflies," *Natural History,* Feb. 1975

Fred A. Urquhart, "Found at Last, the Monarch's Winter Home," *National Geographic,* Aug. 1976.

William G. Wellington, "Tents and Tactics of Caterpillars," *Natural History*, Jan. 1974. Life of the western tent caterpillar.

Larry West, "Check Off the Seasons on This Butterfly Calendar," *National Wildlife*, June 1973

Mark Wexler, "Tropical Gems," *International Wildlife*, Nov. 1974. Colorful moths.

Index